Adventures in History™
THE WAY OF ALEXANDER THE GREAT

Adventures in History™
THE WAY OF ALEXANDER THE GREAT

CHARLES MERCER

Consultant
CORNELIUS C. VERMEULE III
Curator of Classical Art, Museum of Fine Arts, Boston

ibooks
new york
www.ibooks.net

DISTRIBUTED BY SIMON & SCHUSTER

An ibooks, inc. Book

Distributed by Simon & Schuster, Inc.
1230 Avenue of the Americas, New York, NY 10020

"The Battle of Alexander against King Darius" by Pietro'da Cortona courtesy
Erich Lessing/Art Resource, NY

The ibooks World Wide Web Site address is:
http://www.ibooks.net

ISBN: 0-7434-9339-7

First ibooks printing October 2004

10 9 8 7 6 5 4 3 2 1

PRINTED IN THE U.S.A.

CONTENTS

FOREWORD

Throughout the centuries Alexander the Great has fascinated all manner of men all over the world. The results of this universal fascination have been both good and bad: the historic facts of what that handsome, youthful military genius actually did have been blurred; but the works of art that have been created over the ages in an effort to recapture Alexander's spirit now make up one of the world's richest treasuries.

This book is a concerted effort to pull together the scattered images of Alexander and his life, and to present them with all the color and drama characteristic of his time. It is no wonder that the reader gets the impression of a tour through the courts and across the battlefields of the entire ancient world. For that is the way Alexander passed. From his kingdom of Macedon he moved south into classical Greece. Then in one daring leap he crossed into Asia and fought his way down the east coast of the Mediterranean to Egypt, where he was greeted as a god and a pharaoh; after that he advanced to the fabled capitals of the Persian Empire and on to the eastern frontier of the known world—India.

Wherever he went he tried to spread his concept of a world state based on the Greek language, on shared customs, and on a mixture of the races of Europe,

Africa, and Asia. But when death came to him at thirty-two, no one else could hold East and West together. And each of the many lands of his empire then took unto itself what part of him they wanted to keep and revere: in Rome, centuries after Alexander's death, emperors strove to live up to the Alexandrian ideal of divine kingship; in Afghanistan, mountain mothers still frighten their children into good behavior with tales of "Iskander."

Alexander stands forth as the first world ruler to come from Europe. His success, for a time, was breathtaking. How he managed it, how he conducted himself, and what it all led to are questions that challenge and worry men today as we view our own divided world.

CORNELIUS C. VERMEULE III

I

THE FIRST COMMAND

In the summer of 338 B.C., King Philip II of Macedon led his massive army south into the heart of neighboring Greece. From the time he had become king, Philip had been expanding his holdings, overpowering the Greek city-states one by one. Nearly all of Greece was his now; Athens and Thebes were the most vulnerable cities that still remained outside his dominion, but he felt certain that they would also fall. There were good reasons for him to be confident: he was the strongest monarch on the Balkan Peninsula, and his soldiers composed the fiercest and best-trained army that had ever been assembled. He had turned a horde of undisciplined Macedonian peasants—farmers and cattle breeders—into a brilliantly coordinated fighting machine.

On a dusty plain near the village of Chaeronea in central Greece, he halted his soldiers. It was here they would fight their most important battle—against the combined armies of Athens and Thebes, together with allies from nearby Thessaly. Night came, and the Macedonian camp was a scene of clamorous activity as the men prepared for battle. Above the neighing of horses and the harsh shouts of command there rose a strange, persistent chirping, like that of a thousand crickets, as swords and spear tips were honed to razor sharpness. The men slept, but only briefly, for they were awakened long before dawn. They prayed to their gods, gulped water to wash down their ration of bread, and moved out to their battle positions.

Probably none of the soldiers looked fiercer than the King himself that morning as he sat tall on his horse—to the right of the Macedonian lines. Few bore so many battle scars as Philip. An old wound made him limp; a broken collarbone still pained him; and one of his eyes had been gouged from its socket. However, he had one good leg. And with his one good eye he could peer into the receding darkness at the army he had trained. With its Thessalian allies it totaled about 30,000 infantry and 2,000 cavalry. The enemy force was greater by possibly 5,000 men.

As light pierced the sky behind the rocky hills, the Macedonians perceived enemy troops deployed along the mile-wide front. The Athenians were opposite the Macedonian right wing, and the Thebans were on the left. Then, as the rising sun flooded the plain with brightness, a mighty shout rose from the Athenians on Philip's front, and they pressed forward with leveled spears. To their surprise, Philip ordered his right wing to withdraw, and the Athenian advance, moving faster and faster, became a full-scale onslaught.

Suddenly the Macedonian left wing went into action. In command was a blond youth mounted on a black stallion. Handsome and strong, he was Philip's son Alexander, and he had only recently turned eighteen.

Roaring savagely, Alexander's men charged ahead. When they crashed into the waiting Theban wing, the sound must have been like that of a great steel door slamming shut. Spears shivered on shields as the Thebans stubbornly held their line. Then the Macedonians drew short swords and hewed their way into the Theban ranks. Alexander rode with them, leaning from his charger Bucephalus, his sword flashing tirelessly. The Companions, Macedon's select cavalrymen, tried to screen their young prince from the soldiers who flung themselves at him. But he plunged ahead; battle meant nothing less than personal combat to Alexander, even at that age.

Under the pressure of Alexander's charge, the Theban line recoiled and bent back. When the line finally snapped, Alexander wheeled his troops toward the center. Meanwhile, Philip had drawn the Athenians on the right into a trap of low ground. Turning, Philip's wing smashed through the enemy's extended force and it too retreated toward the center. There the famed Sacred Band of Thebes, fighters sworn to die rather than surrender, still fought bravely.

Yet even the strongest steel of Thebes could not withstand the hammer strokes of Alexander on the left and Philip on the right. Every one of the three hundred members of the Sacred Band died fighting. And their Greek allies, who had been in the center, were annihilated.

It was a decisive victory, one that elevated Philip at last as master of all the Greek city-states. The conquest of the Athenians was particularly important, for Athens was esteemed as the cultural center of the world. Philip would try now to bring Athenian artists and scholars into crude Macedon, for he wanted his homeland to be worthy of his new empire. He sent his Theban prisoners into slavery but released all the captured Athenians. He needed the good will of their fellow citizens and the support of their fleet, which constituted the greatest naval power in Greece. So instead of marching into Athens with his victorious army, plundering the city and wreaking destruction, he sent his emissaries there—led by an able general and by his son Alexander.

As the young man rode south from the battlefield on that summer day in 338, he began what was to be a long journey into history. Athens was only the first stop; soon he would look beyond the distant horizons, and all of the known world would be part of his domain.

Over the centuries Alexander, who came to be called

Alexander the Great, has been one of history's most fascinating and controversial men. His life story has been told and retold, yet the true character of the man himself remains a mystery. Dozens of works about him were published by his contemporaries, representing him from different points of view. Only portions of these works exist now, but they were all available in complete form at the close of the first century B.C. They served as the basis of books that five superb historians wrote in the first three centuries after Christ. It is to these men that we owe our knowledge of Alexander: Plutarch, Arrian, Diodorus, Curtius, and Justin.

The story of Alexander, however it may be told, begins with Philip, his father, and his mother, Olympias. Philip was a forthright warrior, a practical man with great military and administrative talents—combined with the lustful appetites and passions of his Macedonian ancestors. Queen Olympias was the orphaned daughter of the ruler of the mountain kingdom of Epirus, which lay near the border of present-day Albania. She claimed, however, to be descended from the Greek warrior Achilles, and she worshiped Dionysus, son of the chief god, Zeus.

Her beauty had attracted Philip when he made her his queen, but her domineering nature soon repelled him. And her powers as an enchantress frightened him, for she charmed snakes and engaged in mystical rites that in Philip's eyes were disgusting. Also, she was without conscience. Soon after Alexander's birth, in midsummer of 356 B.C., Olympias almost convinced her husband that he had not been the infant's father. She insisted that a god was the real parent. This god, she said, was Ammon, or Zeus-Ammon, who had mystic powers of fertility and manifested his presence in shooting stars and thunderbolts.

From the time of his childhood, Olympias instilled in Alexander a fascination with magic, and at an early age he was taught to perform mystic rites. Perhaps more than anything else Olympias was intent on making her son as unlike Philip as possible, for she fought in Alexander everything that might have been inherited from or influenced by his father.

Olympias did not seem to realize—or perhaps she did not care—that her husband was an extraordinary military strategist and a shrewd politician who was trying to bring all of Greece under his leadership. With her selfish, waspish temperament, Olympias could only see Philip's faults: that he drank too much and that he was easily angered, careless with money, and continually falling in love with other women.

Inevitably the estrangement of Philip and Olympias created a strain on Alexander, for he could not please one without offending the other. At an early age he was placed under the tutelage of a relative named Leonidas. A near kinsman of Olympias', Leonidas was so stern in his discipline of the young prince that he would not allow the boy to eat the rich food served at the palace table. In later years, according to Plutarch, Alexander would recall that Leonidas provided him with the best possible diet—"a night march to prepare for breakfast, and a moderate breakfast to create an appetite for supper." Leonidas tried to curb Alexander's instinctive quick temper and trained him to become an exceptional swordsman and athlete—superb at riding, running, hunting, and all competitive games.

Alexander's courage and his powers of observation were apparent when he was still a child. Plutarch describes an incident in which Alexander, at the age of twelve, tamed the black stallion Bucephalus. Philip had planned to buy the horse but changed his mind because the creature seemed too vicious and unmanageable. As Bucephalus was being led away, Philip heard his son remark that an excellent horse was being lost because of a lack of skill and boldness in handling him. Philip inquired somewhat sarcastically if Alexander thought he knew more about managing horses than his elders—to which the boy replied, "I could manage this horse better than others do." Philip accepted this statement as a challenge and wagered the price of the horse that the boy could not live up to his boast.

Cautiously, Alexander took hold of Bucephalus' bridle and turned the powerful animal toward the sun. He had observed that Bucephalus was frightened by the movements of his own shadow. Now, with the shadow behind him, the horse calmed down, and Alexander mounted and slowly drew in the reins. Then when the stallion was completely in his command, Alexander urged him into a gallop. Plutarch says that when the boy finally halted Bucephalus, "his father, shedding tears, it is said, for joy, kissed him as he came down from his horse." Philip bought Bucephalus for his son, and Alexander was the only one who ever rode the creature after that.

In an age of fine horsemen, Alexander grew up to be outstanding. It is generally forgotten that in that day everyone rode bareback. Indeed, the saddle was not introduced until the fourth century A.D., and surviving writings do not mention stirrups until the sixth century. Alexander was equally proficient as a charioteer and often practiced leaping from his chariot as it careened along at top speed.

Although Philip was pleased with Alexander's physical strength and valor, he knew that wisdom was as important as courage in one who would be king. So when Alexander was thirteen, Philip decided to hire a new tutor. The King certainly did not wish to entrust his son's schooling to an ordinary teacher, and some historians speculate that Philip may have feared the continued influence of Leonidas, who was, after all, related to Olympias. At any rate, Philip sent for Aristotle, the wisest man in Greece, to serve as Alexander's tutor.

Aristotle, whose fame has endured as long as that of his royal pupil, was a practical man of the world. Yet as an intellectual he had no equal. The most gifted student of the great philosopher Plato, he is credited with having written between four hundred and a thousand books. He was undistinguished in appearance: small and slight, his deepset eyes gazed out critically from under a wide, wrinkled forehead.

In his writings Aristotle sought to grasp the entire

gamut of human experience and natural phenomena. By his own hard thinking he had formulated the new science of logic. And he was also the first great physical scientist. His findings in physics and biology, for example, stood unchallenged for a thousand years.

Foremost among his achievements as Alexander's tutor was his success in teaching the boy to think logically. He whetted Alexander's curiosity about the natural world and its unknown geography and gave him a lifelong love for the writings of the Greek poet Homer. Aristotle could not erase Olympias' influence, however, and Alexander remained headstrong, superstitious, and highly emotional.

Aristotle was Alexander's tutor for only three years. At the end of that period, when the boy was sixteen, the sounds of battle and his own restlessness and ambition were beginning to lure him onto the stage of history. Philip wanted Alexander to learn the techniques of warfare by serving in the army, and the young prince quickly demonstrated a remarkable aptitude for soldierly skills. Now Philip set him to learning the administration of Macedon, leaving the boy behind in Pella, the Macedonian capital, when he went off to fight the Byzantines. Alexander governed efficiently in his father's absence, and even quelled a Thracian uprising. He rejoined Philip's army—this time as a commander—before the battle of Chaeronea.

After that great Macedonian victory, in which he had played such an important part, Alexander considered himself a man despite his youth. His character had been formed by his mystical mother and his warrior father, by the stern Leonidas and the rational Aristotle. And by the time he left for Athens as his father's ambassador, it can be assumed that his mother had whispered to him her private belief that he was a child of the gods, and therefore unlike other men.

No one knows for certain if Alexander shared his mother's conviction, just as no one knows if Alexander ever really believed he was a god. But as he rode toward Athens on his black horse, Bucephalus, there is reason to suppose that he felt as if he had been singled out for greatness—as indeed he had been.

II

A WOULD-BE KING

When Alexander arrived in Athens in 338 B.C., the city was past the peak of its power, and its cultural life was already on the wane. The rich were growing richer, but the far more numerous poor were sinking deeper into poverty. Athenians, their critics complained, had become soft—hiring mercenaries to substitute for them in battle, watching games instead of playing them.

Yet Alexander, a raw youth from the mountain kingdom of Macedon, must have been impressed when he saw the great city. With its many beautiful temples and public buildings, Athens embodied a culture that was far richer and more advanced than that of rustic Macedon.

Although the defeated Athenians greeted Alexander and his delegation royally, many men saw the Macedonians as bitter enemies. Their leader was Demosthenes, a fluent orator and an unscrupulous politician who was not above slandering people who opposed him or twisting facts to suit his ends. King Philip liked to think of himself as a liberator who would bring peace to the Greeks of Europe and Asia and weld them into a great confederacy. But Demosthenes saw him as an enslaver who threatened to extinguish the flickering light of democracy.

For some time after the battle of Chaeronea, however, the Athenians paid little attention to Demosthenes. Like other Greek city-states, Athens had been exhausted by continual wars among its vying factions. It had tried to unify the discordant Greek states and had failed, as had Sparta and Thebes. Now at last the Macedonians under Philip appeared to be succeeding.

Alexander and his father's representatives came to Athens with an offering of peace. There was one stipulation, however: Philip was to be recognized as the general of all Greece in a war against Persia, the common foe of Greece and Macedon.

The Athenians were astonished—and relieved—for Philip had turned out to be a benign conqueror after all. And they were so pleased that he had left them with a large measure of their freedom that they erected a monument to him, sent him complimentary messages, and entertained Alexander lavishly.

Philip, meanwhile, set out on a triumphal tour of Greece that took the better part of a year. He was received warmly by all but the Spartans, who refused to recognize him as their leader. They even refused to admit him to their city as a guest. When he vowed to show them no mercy if he conquered Sparta, they replied defiantly by repeating the word "if." Reconsidering, he withdrew. Since the Spartans had no allies in Greece, Philip was certain they would be powerless to cause him trouble.

In Corinth, at the close of 338, Philip convened an assembly of representatives from every Greek state except Sparta. Forming them into a general federation, he explained his plans for invading the empire of the Persian Great King, Darius III. Philip hoped merely to "free" the Greek cities that were geographically within the Persian realm, in present-day Turkey, and bring them into his federation. He did not wish to conquer Persia, he said, but he was determined to avenge Persia's invasion of Greece a century and a half earlier.

The federation formed by Philip did not give him absolute power over all the member states. The structure of the organization permitted each state to retain its constitution—but not to change it—and also to maintain a small degree of autonomy. This leniency delighted the representatives at Corinth and won for Philip their pledges of allegiance. Jubilantly they offered him troops to fight the Persians and promised that no Greek would raise a hand against him.

Soon after the meeting at Corinth adjourned, Philip sent a ten-thousand-man advance guard into Persia to set up a bridgehead and attempt to persuade the Asiatic Greeks to secede from the Persian Empire. Once his troops were dispatched, Philip embarked on a campaign of a more personal nature: courtship. The forty-five-year-old Macedonian monarch had fallen in love again—as he had with monotonous frequency since his youth—this time with a girl in her teens. Like the later queen of Egypt, this girl's name was Cleopatra, and she was the niece of Attalus, one of Philip's generals.

Alexander remonstrated with his father, fearing that his own right to the crown would be jeopardized if Philip had a son by Cleopatra. No doubt he was aware of what was being whispered in Philip's court. Many of the King's close advisers were convinced that by his new marriage Philip hoped to change the royal succession. They said that Olympias' continued insistence that Alexander was a god had finally made Philip wonder if the young man really was his son. But they must have realized that since Philip had given Alexander careful training and heavy responsibilities, he still regarded the prince as his heir.

A rift had developed between father and son, however, and Olympias was obviously the cause of it. She did everything possible to make Alexander hostile to Philip. And her continued influence on Alexander helped to underscore the differences between him and his father.

Like every warrior in the army, Philip wore a heavy beard; whereas Alexander insisted on appearing cleanshaven, a startling refinement at the time. Furthermore, Alexander's strength and athletic skill had made him the darling of the young hotbloods in the

Macedonian army; whereas Philip was too battle-weary to equal the boy's vigor. Philip was a sociable man who enjoyed drinking and carousing, and he was doubtless annoyed by Alexander's refusal to join him in his favorite pastimes. His son's aloofness often approached hostility, which only increased Philip's hatred of Olympias. The tension in the royal household reached its peak—and then snapped—when Philip repudiated Olympias as his queen (though not as his wife) and proceeded to marry young Cleopatra, making her the new queen.

In that age absolute monarchs like Philip permitted themselves varying numbers of wives, but only one queen. According to a story told by Plutarch four centuries later, Alexander sat in grim silence at his father's wedding, while the other guests, adhering to custom, drank themselves into a stupor on the banquet couches.

At last Attalus proposed a toast to a child of Philip and Cleopatra's who would be a "lawful successor" to the throne. By this Attalus probably meant that such a child would be completely Macedonian, without the foreign Epirote strain Alexander had inherited from Olympias. But Alexander misunderstood. Enraged at the inference that he was an illegitimate son, he sprang to his feet and hurled his heavy wine cup at Attalus' head. Attalus ducked and threw his own cup at Alexander.

In the pandemonium that followed, Philip staggered from his couch and started toward Alexander with drawn sword. Apparently he intended to kill the young prince. It is equally apparent that he was blind drunk, for he fell and lay stunned in a pool of spilled wine.

Alexander, according to Plutarch, pointed at his father and cried out scornfully that here was a man preparing to pass from Europe to Asia who could not pass safely from one couch to another. Then he strode from the hall.

By dawn the next day he and his mother had left Pella, taking with them a small group of friends and retainers and traveling as fast as they could. Olympias remained with her brother in the capital of Epirus, which was about 120 miles from Pella, while Alexander went on to Illyria.

The family breach might have lasted indefinitely without the intervention of Demaratus of Corinth, an old friend. It was Demaratus, according to Plutarch, who admonished Philip for his concern with Greek unity when his own house was torn by "so many dissensions and calamities." Won over by this argument, Philip sent for his son.

The intrigue that filled the ensuing months surpassed anything that had ever occurred at the Macedonian court. On one side were the restless prince who desired the crown, and the displaced queen, Olympias, who had returned to Pella with him. On the other side were the new, ambitious Queen and her uncle, a shrewd and powerful general. In the middle was the King, trying to placate two wives while fending off pressure from their opposing factions—and dreaming of military glory in Asia.

When Olympias learned that Cleopatra was to give

birth to an offspring of Philip's, she wailed loudly her fears that Alexander would never wear the Macedonian crown. And she was thrown into a panic when Cleopatra bore Philip a son. Plutarch says that when Olympias learned that a young man, Pausanias, had a grudge against Philip, she "encouraged and exasperated the enraged youth to revenge," and he made plans to murder the King. Whether Alexander was aware of the assassination plot is not known, but it is certain that he was almost as desperate as his mother.

Late in the summer of 336, Alexander's sister was married to her uncle, the king of Epirus, in the former Macedonian capital of Aegae. The day after the ceremony, as Philip entered the theater at Aegae, he was stabbed to death by Pausanias. The vengeful young man was in turn slain by Philip's bodyguard before he could escape.

Alexander immediately proclaimed himself King Alexander III of Macedon, while Olympias hurried back to Pella. There, according to some sources, she commanded Cleopatra to hang herself and then personally tossed the young Queen's infant son into a sacrificial fire. It is more probable, however, that Cleopatra and her child were killed a few weeks later in a purge of all who threatened Alexander's rule.

Despite his hasty seizure of the crown, Alexander's succession to the throne was not unchallenged. Some Macedonian nobles favored other candidates. To support their opposition to Alexander they cited his inexperience as a commander, the disturbing and frequently repeated rumor that he was not really Philip's son, and the possibility that he might have helped bring about the death of the King. However, two of Philip's most trusted generals, Antipater and Parmenio, remained loyal to Alexander. The soldiers of the Macedonian army, who adored Alexander, willingly followed the generals' example.

Thus, barely twenty years of age, Alexander came to the throne as the result of violence. As long as he lived he would know little peace.

III

GENERAL OF THE ARMY

The Greeks received the news of Philip's death with jubilation, for it seemed to signal the end of Macedonian dominance and cancel the pledges made to Philip at Corinth. Nearly everyone said that young Alexander could never lead an army into Asia; some doubted that he could even manage to hold on to the Macedonian crown.

In Athens Demosthenes appeared before the Assembly with a garland of flowers on his head and delivered an oration honoring Philip's assassin. But Demosthenes' political enemy Phocion, the great Athenian general and statesman, pointed out astutely that Philip's death merely reduced the Macedonian army by one man. Phocion wisely saw what few others did: that Philip, with his fiercely loyal Macedonians, had created a formidable military machine that would function equally well under the direction of anyone it trusted.

Only one general voiced opposition to Alexander's succession, and that was Attalus, uncle of Cleopatra. At the time of Philip's assassination, Attalus was across the Dardanelles preparing for the anticipated invasion of Persia. Alexander, learning of his dissension, ordered him to be arrested as a traitor and executed. At the same time Alexander began a purge of all who opposed him.

In the first frenzied weeks of his reign, the federation formed by his father was fast dissolving. While Demosthenes was arousing Athens, Thessaly made preparations for a revolt and Sparta loudly asserted its own jealously held freedom of action. Argolis and Elis declared their independence, Ambracia expelled its small Macedonian garrison, and Macedonian troops were barely able to keep the once-conquered Thebans in line. To complicate Alexander's dilemma further, Macedon itself was being menaced by the half-civilized tribes on its frontiers. Thus the invasion of Asia, which obsessed Alexander even more than it had Philip, was necessarily postponed.

Irritated by the delay and angered by the collapse of the League of Corinth, Alexander summoned his generals and ministers to the palace at Pella. There he announced his intention of marching through Greece and binding the confederation of city-states by the force of his army. His advisers warned against this action, urging Alexander first to secure his position at home. But he scorned their counsel and let them know that he was, unalterably, his own man, not theirs. He was no longer shy and aloof, as he had been as a boy. Almost overnight, it seemed, he had become outspoken—a man of decision.

It would be an exaggeration to call Alexander a tactical genius at the outset of his career. Yet in his first military move after becoming king, he displayed an extraordinary cleverness and a talent for surprise. He did not lead his thirty-thousand-man army directly into the center of unrest in neighboring Thessaly. Instead he avoided the logical approach and slipped down along the rocky coast, probably by night. Much of the time he had to follow goat tracks that had been widened by engineers working hurriedly ahead of his army.

When the Macedonians emerged from the craggy hills into the extreme southeast corner of Thessaly, the bewildered Thessalians to the north realized that they had been cut off from the aid of central Greece, and they submitted meekly to Alexander's leadership.

Then Alexander and his army marched swiftly south, defiled through the pass of Thermopylae, and finally camped under the walls of Thebes, where the Macedonian garrison had been having difficulty holding back the restless inhabitants. Athens, hardly more than a two-day march away, was thrown into terror, and no one could have been more terrified than Demosthenes. When, with fitting irony, the Assembly named him to head a peace mission to Alexander,

Demosthenes was so consumed with fear that upon reaching the Theban border he scuttled back to Athens.

Why did the Macedonian army provoke such terror? In the first place, it was a truly professional army composed of specialists who remained in continuous service. When not on the battlefield it maintained its toughness through training, drilling, and marching. Secondly, the soldiers, proud of being Macedonians, had exceedingly high morale.

Before Philip reorganized the army, the infantry phalanx—footsoldiers marching close together in a rectangular formation—had been the chief arm of assault. The phalanx had always been used like a battering ram for only one purpose: to rupture the enemy front. Philip retained the phalanx and even strengthened it by increasing its depth to sixteen ranks. But he and Alexander employed it primarily to frighten their enemies. The confusion caused by its advance was the signal for an attack by the potent Macedonian cavalry. Charging in close formation on their wiry ponies, the sword-swinging horsemen were invincible.

In addition to cavalry and heavy infantry for drawn battle, Philip used light cavalry and light infantry armed with bows for scouting. At the same time he developed an astonishing variety of catapults, which were the artillery of that time. And he set his newly established corps of engineers to work improving the siege train, which brought together arms and equipment for attacking walled cities.

First and most important of these weapons was the

battering ram for smashing through locked doors or closed gates. It was a huge wooden beam whose head was encased in iron. It was pushed on wheels by men who were protected from enemy arrows by portable rawhide shelters.

Among other essential elements of the siege train were siege towers that could be rolled up to a fortification and made tall enough so that men could scale the walls. There were catapults used to hurl burning spears or pebbles and powered by twisted skeins of hair, and larger catapults called ballistae that were fashioned like huge crossbows and could throw stones weighing about fifty pounds.

But the great powerhouse of the Macedonian army was still the infantry phalanx—composed of hard, indefatigable fellows of medium height and wiry build. They carried fourteen-foot spears which they used for thrusting instead of throwing; the extra length gave them at least a 50 percent advantage over the nine-foot spears used by their opponents. They were also armed with short swords and light, circular shields and they wore breastplates, leggings, and helmets. On long marches they usually slung their heavy helmets over one shoulder and donned broad-brimmed hats. To their enemies they were crude and bestial, but to Alexander they were beloved for their qualities of will and courage, and for the strength that enabled them to endure incredible hardships.

It was fear of these soldiers, rather than any personal magnetism of Alexander's that brought the Greek states tumbling back into the shaky federation. Alexander, like his father before him, called a conference at Corinth to which every state but Sparta sent representatives. The federation members promised to be peaceful, named Alexander their captain-general, and no doubt expressed relief among themselves when he made plans to lead his army quietly back to Macedon.

Before returning home, however, Alexander paid a visit to the temple of Apollo at Delphi to receive a prophecy from the Delphic oracle. According to tradition, the prophecies, or oracles, of the god Apollo were given forth from the temple by a priestess known as the Pythia. She sat on a circular slab atop a gilded wooden tripod. Beneath the tripod was a deep gash in the earth from which pungent vapors arose to excite her into a state of ecstasy. In this state, the Pythia's words were gibberish—hysterical ravings which trained prophets translated into language that could be understood by whoever had sought the prophecies.

Alexander's visit to the Delphic oracle was in a pattern of behavior that continued throughout his life. Before each important undertaking he sacrificed to the gods and concerned himself with omens and portents of what would happen. After the event he expressed his gratitude to whatever gods he felt might have aided him and tried to appease the gods he believed he had offended. Although Alexander's motives may have been selfish and far from the realm of piety, he gave the impression of being as deeply concerned with religion as with war. Eventually he used religion as well as arms to enforce peace on conquered peoples.

The impetuous haste that was part of his character was evident at Delphi. He arrived at the temple on one of the days that were forbidden for prophecy and learned that the elderly woman who served as the Pythia was resting at home. In vain the temple priests tried to explain to him that it would take a few days to set the oracle's powers in motion. Declaring that he had no time to waste in waiting, Alexander hurried off to the Pythia's house, bursting in on the astonished woman to ply her with questions.

Alexander was desperately curious to know if all would go well on his forthcoming invasion of the Persian Empire. Doubtless the Pythia told him his inquiry was unprecedented and impossible to answer on the spot. Possibly he responded with good-natured flattery, for he had a charming way with elderly women. Or perhaps, as Plutarch describes the incident, Alexander drew her into the temple by force. At any rate, she finally gave him an answer. "My son," she said in exasperation, "thou art invincible."

Delighted, Alexander now rode home to Pella. There, to his vexation, he realized that once again he would have to postpone his assault on the Persian Empire. Although he accepted the oracle's promise of invincibility in a war against Persia, he knew he could not succeed without all of Greece solidly behind him. And at this time, inland tribes as far north as the Danube were in revolt. Unless quelled they would menace his home base of Macedon the moment his army began its march to Asia.

The early spring of 335 found him sloshing through

melting snow in the lofty Balkans. The strength of his army is not known, but it probably numbered less than ten thousand because the mountain terrain made it difficult to keep many troops well supplied. Alexander was acting as his own field commander and purposely must have left his seasoned generals behind in Macedon. One can imagine that he wished to demonstrate his own military capability, for he had not yet fought a battle as king of Macedon and captain-general of all Greece.

From the time he assumed command he knew that the success of the Macedonian army on the battlefield would be determined by his leadership. He knew too that he had to be an example to his troops, for they watched his every movement. To bolster their confidence, and perhaps to reinforce his own, he made a habit of taking his helmet off when he visited or inspected his troops on the battlefield. Bareheaded, he showed that he too was vulnerable; they loved him for this human touch and redoubled their determination to fight and to follow wherever he led.

When the Macedonians reached the Shipka Pass, only the astuteness and quick thinking of Alexander prevented a disastrous rout. The pass was held by Thracian rebels who had arranged their carts to form a stockade on a hill above the Macedonians. Alexander was certain that the Thracians planned to roll the carts down the hill as his men attacked. So he ordered his advancing infantry to open ranks and form lanes through which the carts could pass. Where the slope was not smooth and this action was impossible, he had his men lie down under the protective cover of their interlocked shields. Then, just as Alexander had anticipated, the Thracian carts were turned loose and they thundered down the hill. They passed through Alexander's open ranks and bounded over the men lying beneath the shields, leaving only a few casualties behind them. Rising, the Macedonians continued their uphill advance, scattered the Thracians, and took the pass.

This was not a crucial engagement—hardly more than a skirmish—but it demonstrated Alexander's ability to improvise tactics under unique conditions. Again and again as he marched toward the Danube he showed his tactical cunning and the ability to win battles without wasting the power of his vaunted heavy phalanxes. When, for example, a large force of Triballians hid themselves within the denseness of a wooded glen, Alexander held back his cavalry and sent forward a thin line of infantry archers to act as decoys. The ruse worked perfectly. The Triballians sallied out to destroy the archers, who dispersed as the Macedonian cavalry emerged from concealment and smashed the charging enemy. Arrian says that in this engagement three thousand Triballians were slain, compared to a loss of but fifty-one Macedonians. These figures may be exaggerated. It is known for a fact, however, that the Macedonians took few prisoners—and those few were sold into slavery, with the profits divided among the troops.

At the Danube River, which winds its way through eastern Europe, the Macedonians boarded a small fleet of galleys that Alexander had ordered to sail up from Byzantium by way of the Black Sea. But the galleys could not negotiate the Danube's treacherous currents and were forced to turn back. Alexander and his men were left chafing on the south bank of this mighty river that formed the northern border of the known world. Once again he improvised. He used pieces of wood and leather tent covers stuffed with hay to make rafts and then ferried a force of fifteen hundred cavalry and four thousand infantry across the river in a single night. According to Arrian, the Macedonians reached the northern bank at "a spot where the corn stood high." Then, concealed by these crops, they surprised and scattered the tribesmen who had gathered in force to bar their way.

Alexander's success in crossing the Danube without bridging it produced great strategic results. The stunned northern tribes—even those as distant as the Adriatic Sea—thought it a superhuman feat and sent emissaries to beg for Alexander's friendship. And not for fifty years did any northern tribe try to invade Greece.

Soon after the campaign at the Danube ended, Alexander learned that the Illyrians had revolted. They had seized the Macedonian fortress of Pelion, which dominated the Devol River valley in what is now Albania, and thus they commanded the western route to Macedon.

Alexander marched swiftly southward and ranged his army around the fortress, preparing to besiege it. Suddenly he discovered that his troops had been surrounded by an even larger force of Illyrians. In his overeagerness to recapture Pelion, Alexander had made an error in judgment; the besieger had now become the besieged.

Hemmed in by superior forces, his supplies low, Alexander again confronted disaster. There was no orthodox military maneuver that would extricate the Macedonians from this trap. So Alexander conceived an unorthodox maneuver. On the plain between the fortress and the enemy troops that surrounded him, he set his entire army to performing intricate drill maneuvers. Forward and about, obliquely and by the flanks, the infantry tramped and the cavalry pranced, while the Illyrians on the surrounding hills drifted closer to gape at the splendid show.

Perhaps they thought the Macedonians were performing a grotesque dance of death; that is probably what Alexander hoped. Actually his men were simply stalling for time, hoping to catch their enemy off guard. And when they did, they burst through the Illyrians' line of defense, then turned and pretended to strike. The Illyrians retreated in confusion, and while Alexander's siege engines went into action to hold off a counterattack, his men withdrew hurriedly to a refuge some distance from the fortress.

Three days later, at nightfall, Alexander led a surprise raid on the Illyrian camp and routed it. Destroying the fortress at Pelion, the Illyrians headed for the mountains—with the Macedonians in full pursuit. There, in a skirmish with the enemy, Alexander was struck down by a blow so severe that it nearly broke his neck. Soon a rumor began to spread through Greece that he had been killed.

Demosthenes, addressing the Athenian Assembly, exploited this rumor. He heaped praise on the Persians and made a strong and impassioned plea for a Theban revolt against Alexander. As one Assembly member later expressed it, he was so eloquent that he "all but showed the corpse of Alexander there on the rostrum before our eyes."

Far from being a corpse, Alexander became an angry avenger when, in the far-off mountains, he learned that Demosthenes' tongue was wagging again and that Thebes had closed the Macedonian garrison in its citadel. Fearing that Athens and Sparta and other city-states would unite in revolt against him, Alexander turned his troops toward Thebes. He and his men covered some three hundred miles in fourteen days—fording rivers, climbing mountains, and hacking through thick forests. Arriving at the Theban gates, Alexander offered amnesty to all who would come out and join him.

When the Thebans replied with jeers, Alexander announced that he would attack the city. But before he could lay plans for the siege, a body of his troops ambushed a Theban outpost and chased it through a gate into the city. Fearing that his men might be stranded where they would be outnumbered, Alexander brought up the rest of his army, and they forced their way through the open gate.

There followed one of the most savage scenes in the history of Greece. The Thebans fought desperately in the narrow streets, across the roofs of buildings, even in the temples. But they were no match for the Macedonians, who seemed to have gone blood-mad. Women and children were not spared as the Macedonians killed and pillaged. Alexander lost about 500 men; whereas some 6,000 Thebans were killed and more than 30,000 taken prisoner. All those captured who could not prove they had opposed the rebellion were immediately sold into slavery.

Alexander noticed that among the prisoners awaiting judgment was an attractive, well-dressed woman with her children at her side. He learned that she was accused of murdering an officer—a Thracian, she said, who had broken into her home. She was unrepentant as she described to Alexander how she had lured the officer to the well in which she said her jewelry was hidden. Then when he stooped to extract the treasure, she had pushed him into the well and tossed stones on him, killing him.

When Alexander asked her who she was, the woman said she was the sister of the man who had commanded the Thebans against his father at Chaeronea. Then as she stood before Alexander, seemingly unmoved and waiting for her death sentence, he ordered his men to release her and escort her and her children free of the Macedonian lines.

This action must have raised a few eyebrows among Alexander's contemporaries. For, according to the British historian Sir William Tarn, an expression of pity then "was unmanly, and best left to poets and philosophers." Alexander was capable of extreme cruelty, as were other rulers of his time, but the partic-ular quality that distinguished him most clearly from his fellow men was compassion. And his kindness toward women was almost without precedent.

After the Theban prisoners had been disposed of, Alexander ordered that the entire city be destroyed—all except the temples and the house of the poet Pindar. The destruction was carried out to the music of flutes.

If Alexander had destroyed Thebes solely to shock the Greeks into succumbing to his leadership, then his purpose was fulfilled. The Greeks cringed in terror at the destruction of Thebes, and every state but Sparta made humble gestures of peace. The panic-stricken Athenians, fearing the brutality of Alexander's revenge, sent their foremost statesman, Phocion, to intercede for them. Alexander promised Phocion that no harm would come to Athens. He asked merely that Athens banish one man, Charidemus, who had been fomenting rebellion against Macedon. Even Demos-thenes succeeded in escaping banishment. Although Alexander is not credited with having had a sense of humor, apparently he displayed one at this time. He said that it would be sufficient punishment if Demos-thenes were forced to be silent and retire from politics.

Now all of Greece and the lands stretching to the Danube were in the grasp of Alexander and his army. At last he could undertake his great adventure.

IV

THE MARCH INTO ASIA

One April morning in 334, Alexander of Macedon led his fighting force out of Pella, never to return. The night before, the twenty-two-year-old ruler had presided over a farewell banquet, said goodbye to Olympias, and appointed his loyal general Antipater to serve as regent of Macedon in his absence.

The army that fell into line behind him and took the road west toward the strait of the Dardanelles numbered little more than thirty thousand infantry and five thousand cavalry. Alexander's elderly advisers knew him to be impulsive; this time some may have thought him completely reckless. For he planned to put his relatively small host into the field against the

Persians, who, it was reported, could raise a million men-at-arms.

Alexander had rejected all advice to wait, however. And he had refused to marry and have an heir before undertaking the invasion. To launch his venture he had been forced to borrow money, for his royal treasury was empty. Indeed, he and his army had rations for only one month. But they marched swiftly, purposefully, covering the 350 miles to the port of Sestos in twenty days. From Sestos the coast of Asia lay less than a mile away, a brief boat trip across the Dardanelles.

Dressed in full armor and wearing a white-plumed battle helmet, Alexander stood beside the helmsman of the royal galley so that he could say he had guided the vessel to Asia. Midway across the strait, a sacrificial bull that had been tethered to a temporary altar at the prow of the galley was slaughtered as an offering to Poseidon, the Greek god of the sea. Alexander poured wine into the waves from a golden goblet and then tossed the goblet after it as a further gesture of respect. After stepping ashore, one of his first acts was to visit Troy to anoint and crown with garlands the tomb of his mythical ancestor Achilles.

By such ceremonies Alexander indicated that he did not think of himself as simply another general commencing just another campaign. With his highly developed sense of the dramatic, he seems to have been telling himself, his soldiers, and the world at large that he was beginning a fateful and historic mission. Scholars of history do not agree on what

Alexander considered this mission to be. However, Sir William Tarn insists that Alexander invaded Persia because "he never thought of not doing it; it was his inheritance." Yet no one today can guess how far he planned to go; probably no one knew precisely what was in his mind, even at the time.

The Persian Empire reached from Egypt to the Black and Caspian seas—from the Mediterranean to the Indus River. A century and a half before Alexander's birth, Persia's King Darius I had molded this empire from many nations, and from millions of people who were not united by race, religion, or a common language. That Darius could bind this mixture of peoples and cultures into a single empire was a credit to his administrative genius.

First he had to win his subjects' loyalty. Darius wisely did this by advancing a policy of tolerance. He chose to respect the rights and privileges of each racial and national group in his domain and took care to honor their traditions and customs. He ruled over each people in the role of their traditional leader—as a pharaoh to the Egyptians, for example, and as a king to the Babylonians.

Then he had to rule. For the purposes of administration, Darius divided his empire into twenty provinces, or satrapies, each under a viceroy, or satrap, whose primary functions were to collect tribute money and maintain law and order. Realizing that ambitious viceroys would strive eventually for independence from the central Persian authority, Darius kept them under close surveillance and maintained a strong standing army of his own. The core of this army was a force of ten thousand infantrymen called the Immortals.

Darius seemed to feel a great civilizing mission among the peoples he and his predecessors had conquered. The sweep of his program of improvements touched all but a small part of his empire. He had a large inland canal built from the Nile River to the Red Sea, established superb harbors and huge water basins to irrigate arid land, built roads and bridges to speed up troop movement, and attempted to send ships around Africa.

The excellent military roads Darius constructed provided a swift means of transportation and communication. Normally, for example, the fifteen-hundred-mile journey from Sardis to Susa took ninety days. But royal couriers, supplied with fresh horses at posting houses along the way, covered the distance in seven days.

It was by this means that Darius III, who had come to the throne in 336, learned so quickly of Alexander's landing in Asia.

Darius III, who bore the traditional title of Great King, was a capable soldier, but he lacked the genius of the first Darius. By the time Darius III had gained control of the empire, Persian power was beginning to wane. In some respects the empire was operating on its past glory. The Immortals had disbanded, and although Persia still controlled the seas, its army depended largely on Greek mercenaries. In theory,

Darius had the forces of each viceroy at his disposal, but many of these men were unreliable and corrupt.

True, the empire still maintained good roads and its administrative machinery was as efficient as ever. But these resources could be as valuable to a bold and wise aggressor as they were to a defender.

Although the sinews of the empire had softened, its nerves were still sound. And it reacted promptly to Alexander's invasion. A Persian force gathered by Spithridates, the viceroy of Lydia and Ionia, and Arsites, satrap of Phrygia, took up a defensive position behind the shallow Granicus River seventy miles east of Alexander's camp at Arisbe.

According to Arrian, the Persian army consisted of twenty thousand cavalrymen and nearly as many mercenary Greek infantrymen led by Memnon, the Rhodian Greek general who also commanded the Persian fleet. Modern historians believe that most of these mercenaries were assigned to the ships, instead of the infantry. Thus it is likely that the Persian land force was smaller than Alexander's.

Memnon urged the Persians to withdraw before Alexander, laying waste the country behind them, and then to maneuver to the coast and employ their powerful fleet to invade Macedon. But Spithridates and Arsites rejected Memnon's advice, despite its wisdom, for they were certain that the Persians' fighting skill was superior to that of the Macedonians.

The Persians were as proud and as brave as the Macedonians. Their traditional weapon was he bow, their striking arm the cavalry, and their leaders took great delight in personal combat. But at the battle of Granicus their pride and personal bravery became their undoing.

When Alexander led his army to the banks of the river on that spring afternoon, his confidence soared. For he saw immediately that the Persians had made a grave tactical error. They had massed their cavalry along the steep eastern bank, where it could not charge, and had withdrawn their potent Greek mercenary infantry to the rear.

The Persians planned to kill Alexander and drive away his then demoralized army. They had given little thought to the problem of defending their soil.

Certainly the Persian soldiers must have appeared invincible; they were heavily armored, they had a massive body of horsemen, and their love of bright colors must have been displayed in an impressive panoply dazzling to Western eyes. Yet Alexander wanted to begin the battle without delay and take advantage of the faulty distribution of the Persian troops. It is also possible that Alexander wanted to attack at once because the declining afternoon sun was in the enemy's eyes. Once again, to gain a victory, Alexander was improvising an unexpected plan of attack.

The Persian leaders recognized him easily because of the brightness of his armor, and they watched him marshaling his forces along the riverbank. Although they could observe his every action, they could not penetrate his plan. What little they understood of it must have seemed vague and confused. Actually, the unorthodox battle plan had been carefully conceived, and Alexander executed it perfectly.

In the center of his line he placed his powerful infantry phalanxes, with a wing of cavalry at either end. Alexander manipulated these cavalry wings like the fists of a boxer. At first he withheld the left, commanded by Parmenio, and jabbed with his light cavalry on the right. As the Persian cavalrymen warded off this blow, their commanders doubtless expected Alexander to release a decisive punch with his left. But Alexander deceived them. Still withholding his left, he launched the decisive them. Still withholding his left, he launched the decisive attack on the right, leading his own mounted Companions. They galloped across the Granicus—through a lane of steel formed by light cavalry and heavy infantry—and drove toward the heart of the Persian left wing where the enemy generals were gathered.

As the Companions burst through the Persians' front ranks, Alexander's spear was shattered. Another was provided by Demaratus the Corinthian, the man who once settled a feud between Alexander and his father. The moment Alexander took the sword he was attacked by Darius' son-in-law Mithridates. Alexander drove his spear into his attacker's face, killing him. Then Rhoesaces, another Persian commander, struck Alexander on the head with a battle-axe and cut away half of Alexander's helmet and one of its white plumes.

Although stunned by the blow, Alexander knocked Rhoesaces to the ground and plunged his spear through the man's breastplate and into his heart. Spithridates advanced behind Alexander, his sword raised for the kill. But Cleitus, one of the Companions, lunged forward and with one mighty slash severed Spithridates' arm at the shoulder; it fell to the ground with the sword still in hand.

While the fighting around Alexander grew more intense, Parmenio's left-wing cavalry attacked, and the armored infantry slammed its solid phalanxes into the crumbling Persian front. Under these fresh onslaughts the remaining Persians wavered, withdrew in confusion, and finally fled.

Alexander did not pursue them far. He turned instead upon the Greek mercenaries who had scarcely been engaged. Surrounded and knowing they would receive no quarter—for Alexander wished to make an example of them to discourage other Greeks from fighting for Persia—the mercenaries fought valiantly against wave after wave of Macedonian infantry and cavalry. Two thousand Greeks surrendered finally, and when darkness came the battle ended.

Among the dead on the field were a son-in-law and a brother-in-law of Darius—in addition to several princes and viceroys, including Spithridates. The cavalry commander Arsites committed suicide, but Memnon, who had led the Greek mercenaries, escaped. The historian Diodorus puts the Persian losses at 12,000 slain and 20,000 captured, as compared to only 150 Macedonians dead. Doubtless these figures too are exaggerations. Alexander, like many other commanders, enjoyed boasting that his army had inflicted huge losses on its enemies at but a slight cost to itself.

Alexander's conduct after his triumph at the Granicus reveals much about his nature, which seems to have been a peculiar blend of kindness and brutality.

After the battle he visited each of his wounded soldiers and helped his doctors prescribe for them, for he professed almost as much interest in the healing art as in the art of war. However, he showed almost no concern for the captured Greek mercenaries. He had them herded together and sent to join the chain gangs of Macedon, for in bearing arms against Alexander they had demonstrated their refusal to recognize him as the overlord of all Greece. The Thebans among the captured mercenaries were set free, however, for Alexander still recalled his destruction of Thebes with a sense of guilt.

Most of the rich Persian booty was divided among Alexander's men because, though thoroughly disciplined, they expected wealth as a reward for marching into Asia. Alexander took little booty himself; his personal wants were simple and few. But some of the choicest captured items were sent home to Olympias.

Perhaps his most significant gesture, following the battle, was the one made to the city of Athens: a gift of three hundred captured suits of Persian armor, accompanied by this inscription: "Alexander, son of Philip, and all the Greeks except the Spartans present this offering from the spoils taken from the foreigners inhabiting Asia." This was almost his last public reference to himself as Philip's son. Henceforth he would deny the influence of his father, for he no longer wished to stand in the shadow of any man. His gift and the inscription that went with it indicate that Alexander still yearned for the admiration of Athens and wanted to be considered a Greek. He knew, of course, that most Athenians held him in contempt as an outlander from Macedon.

Now that Alexander had established his Asian beach-head, he took immediate steps to protect it and at the same time maintain a swift and easy access to the sea. He not only had to occupy the west coast of Asia Minor but he also had to leave peaceful and friendly countries behind him as he advanced. Important cities lay along the Aegean and Mediter-ranean seacoasts like rich pearls strung along the water. Many had been founded by Greek colonizers from Lydia and Ionia who had left their crowded countries centuries before to spread their influence to the distant shores of the Mediterranean.

Alexander's approach to these cities of Asia Minor was politic and also unique for its time. He announced that he had come as a liberator to free them from Persian bondage and restore their ancient Greek prerogatives. He also offered them a measure of self-determination, for he depended upon their friendship to consolidate his empire. Foremost in his thoughts, it seems clear, was the concept of Greek unity that Philip had pursued.

To achieve this unity Alexander knew he would have to create an alliance with all the anti-Persian factions he encountered. And he would have to stress to them the benefits to be gained from merging with his greater, all-encompassing empire—even if such an alliance meant subordinating their powers to the overall power of his rule.

Ironically, his idea was similar to that held by the founders of the Persian Empire. However, as the first Western leader to try to make the idea a large-scale reality, Alexander earned a significant place in political history. His foreign policy was based on the premise that liberty and a free choice of government should be awarded to all conquered subjects. However, the Alexandrian concept of liberty had strict limitations; obviously the conqueror would never grant a defeated government so much power that it could threaten or challenge his authority.

In Asia Minor the people of the cities of Sardes and Ephesus greeted Alexander warmly. It is not clear what freedoms, if any, he restored to them, for he placed his own men in power under administrative systems similar to those of the Persians. In Ephesus, however, he did make a grand gesture that must have delighted the citizens. Despite his great need for money, he ordered the completion of a new temple of Artemis, which had burned mysteriously on the day he was born. And he specified that the tribute money the Ephesians had been paying each year to Darius should henceforth be used for the temple's up-keep. Certainly this gesture reflected his concern with religion. Possibly it also expressed his ideas of national freedom.

Heading south once again, Alexander came to the

important port city of Miletus, which was the center of the Ionian Greek civilization. There, before the city's barred gates, he came to realize that few Greeks shared his dream of national unity. To the Milesians, as to millions of their contemporaries, Alexander was not a great hero. Rather, he was an upstart Balkan warrior, another would-be conqueror whose purpose was to interrupt the established order of their lives.

Miletus was a thriving commercial center, its people intelligent and aggressive. It had been colonized by Ionians from Attica in about 1000 B.C., and by the sixth century B.C. had become the wealthiest city in the Greek world. Milesian athletes acquitted themselves well in the Olympic Games, and well-heeled aristocrats patronized philosophy and the arts. By every standard except that of military might, Milesian life was superior to anything that existed in Macedon.

When the Macedonians rattled their swords outside the walls of Miletus, emissaries came out and told Alexander that if he would leave their city alone, it would remain neutral in the war. Angered by their indifference to his aims, Alexander replied that he had not come to share with others—but to take all. The Milesians chose to fight.

Alexander took the city after a desperate battle, and his army slaughtered its defenders mercilessly. To aid his cause he recruited three hundred Greek mercenaries who had found refuge on an offshore island, expecting to be killed or sold into slavery by the Macedonians. This was a significant change in policy, indicating that Alexander had grown more realistic and now knew he could not continue to regard all the Greeks who opposed him as traitors. Henceforth he would pardon those Greek mercenaries who agreed to join his army and serve him.

With Miletus firmly in his grasp, Alexander's overseas base was at last completed. He controlled the eastern shore of the Aegean, and from it he could communicate with Greece by way of the islands that were arranged like stepping stones between the two coasts.

One of his next moves was to divide his army, sending part of it north under the leadership of Parmenio, his second-in-command, to take up strategic winter quarters at Gordium, which lay southwest of the modern Turkish city of Ankara. There on the great trade route out of northern Persia, which the ancient historian Herodotus called the Royal Highway, Parmenio could check any aggressive movement Darius might attempt.

But the Persians did not act in haste. Their slowness to retaliate after the defeat at the Granicus underscores their leisurely temperament as well as a decline in their incentive to fight. A huge army was slowly being assembled during this time, however. And when it eventually met Alexander on a narrow plain at Issus, the ensuing battle was like a fight to the death between an elephant and a tiger.

While Darius was drawing together his forces, Alexander was prowling southern Asia Minor. This was rugged country—mountainous, cleft by twisting gorges and valleys, often fiercely cold. But it held for

Alexander the lure of combat and conquest. He did not fight great battles there, but he engaged in innumerable skirmishes. The size of a conflict made no difference to him. His joy in battle was uncontained, and his method was always the same: to lead the decisive attack personally and seek out the enemy leaders—charging them with spears leveled at their faces.

Nearly always at his side was his closest friend, Hephaestion. He and Alexander were like brothers, say the ancient authorities, sharing their confidences, the same tent, even the same dishes. No physical description of Hephaestion survives, but it can be assumed that he looked much like Alexander, young and handsome. Once, according to legend, when a captured princess came before them, she gave obeisance to Hephaestion, mistaking him for Alexander. Far from being annoyed, Alexander seemed delighted by her error.

By all the probabilities of chance, Alexander should have already lost his life in battle. Yet, at this time, he was brought closest to death by illness rather than warfare. He had marched north to Gordium early in the winter of 333, joined forces with Parmenio, and had accompanied the Macedonians south in the late spring or early summer to seize the commercial center of Tarsus. When the army descended from the temperate mountains onto the humid plain, Alexander plunged into the cold Cydnus River for a swim. Shortly afterward he was overcome by a fever which may have been a form of typhoid.

For days his life was in danger, and the army seems to have been paralyzed with fear, for its every action, its every move, was dependent on Alexander's leadership. It is possible to imagine the wave of rejoicing that swept through the ranks when news came that Alexander had survived the fever—and the purgatives and bleedings that characterized the medical practice of his time.

The writings of Arrian and Plutarch indicate that while Alexander was gravely ill, Parmenio sent him a message to warn that his trusted chief physician, Philip, had been bribed by Darius to poison him. As Philip handed Alexander a purgative, so the story goes, Alexander handed Philip the message from Parmenio. Plutarch says that while Philip read the warning, Alexander drank the potion, looking "cheerful and open, to show his kindness to and confidence in his physician." Even if exaggerated, the story does illustrate the fact that Alexander's confidence in his friends was as yet unshakable.

In the summer of 333, while Alexander was securing his bases and clearing his lines of communication, a huge army under Darius was moving up the Euphrates River from Babylonia. Only a calculated guess can be made of its exact size. Arrian and Plutarch say it numbered 600,000 men; Justin and Diodorus say 500,000; Curtius estimates its strength at 300,000. Considering the size of the field on which it finally came to battle, one might reasonably assume that its strength was well over 100,000. Alexander's army, weakened by the toll of summer fever and depleted by the garrison forces that had been left at its bases, apparently now numbered less than 30,000.

Creeping along the winding Euphrates, the advancing Persians probably looked more like a migration than an army on the march. Members of the royal family and thousands of women moved along with the troops. Darius himself traveled in high style; even his royal treasury accompanied him, at least at first.

Early in October Alexander and his Macedonians marched south and then east in search of the Persians. Boldly, Alexander sought Darius on the plains. This was a mistake, although it seemed logical that Darius would choose to fight on the flat lands where his enormous cavalry could more easily envelope the outnumbered Macedonians.

It was no doubt with considerable chagrin that Alexander learned that Darius, in an unexpected move, had abandoned the plains for the hills. Now the Persian army stood behind Alexander, cutting him off from his home base—and from his supplies and reinforcements. In isolating his adversary, Darius had shown strategic wisdom, but in choosing to fight on hilly terrain, he had been foolish.

Realizing that their retreat had been blocked, the Macedonians experienced widespread panic. Alexander reacted quickly, wheeling them around. They poured back over the hills and onto the narrow field of Issus, near Alexandretta, close to the present-day border between Turkey and Syria. There they engaged the Persians on a fighting front that extended only a mile and a half from the hills to the Mediterranean Sea.

This was hardly enough space for Darius to maneuver his great cavalry, and thus it favored the vastly out-numbered Macedonians.

At the start of the battle Alexander deployed his army in its traditional order. His left was anchored where the sea splashed his men's feet; his right was pinned against the hills; and his heavy phalanxes were in the center. After securing his flanks, he began a savage and incisive attack against Darius' headquarters in the center of the Persian line.

Leading the Companion cavalry from the right wing, he hewed his way through the Persian ranks until he was on the point of reaching Darius himself. Then an incredible thing happened: just as victory seemed within Alexander's grasp, his supposedly indomitable phalanxes in the center began to fall back, presumably pushed by the force of overwhelming numbers.

At this moment Alexander once again demonstrated his greatness as a military leader. He shifted his own attack to the left and fell on the mercenary troops who were assaulting his infantrymen. His attack relieved them of pressure, and they rallied. If, instead of turning, he had continued his attack and tried to reach Darius, the phalanxes might have been destroyed and the battle inevitably lost.

Meantime a cry passed through the Persian ranks that Darius had fled. It seemed unlikely that he would have pulled back yet; reputedly he was a brave man, and despite the Macedonians' shattering charge, the battle at this stage was very much in his favor. But as the rumor persisted and continued to spread, confusion and panic gripped the Persian forces. They fell back, demoralized. Then Darius did flee. And all of his men who could extricate themselves raced after him into the hills. Alexander was victorious once more.

V

BY LAND AND BY SEA

Nightfall saved Darius from capture as he galloped into the hills. Alexander, who led the pursuit despite a painful thigh wound, at last turned back to the battlefield. There he found that his men, who had been pillaging the Persian camp, had reserved Darius' tent for him. It had splendid furnishings, says Plutarch, and treasures of silver and gold. Alexander went inside and removed his armor. "Let us go and wash off the sweat of battle in the bath of Darius," he said to one of his Companions, who replied: "Not so, but rather in that of Alexander." Then when Alexander saw the tubs and basins, pitchers and caskets—all made of gold—and sniffed the fragrant odors of rare ointments and perfumes, he said to his followers, "This, it seems, is royalty."

On his way to supper that night he learned that among the Persian prisoners captured after the battle were Darius' mother, Sisygambis; his wife, Statira; and two daughters. Alexander sent word to them that Darius was not dead and that they would be treated fairly and cordially.

The Persian casualty rate at Issus was enormous. The principal authorities place the losses at more than 100,000—as opposed to but a few hundred for Alexander. This appears to be a gross exaggeration, however, for it is known that 2,000 Greek mercenaries and countless numbers of Persians fled with Darius, while 8,000 other Greek mercenaries escaped through the mountains and later took ship to Egypt.

Not long after the battle, Alexander sent the reliable and tireless Parmenio and a part of his army to Damascus to seize Darius' field treasury. Parmenio brought back not only a huge sum of money and great hordes of valuable objects but also the wives and families of many notable Persians who then came under Alexander's protection.

Soon Alexander received a letter from Darius himself in which the Persian monarch pleaded for the release of his family—in exchange for a friendly alliance with Alexander. According to Arrian, Alexander replied: "I am, by gift of the gods, in possession of your land. . . . Come to me then, and ask for your mother, wife, and children. . .For whatever you ask for, you will receive; and nothing shall be denied you.

But for the future, whenever you send to me, send to me as the king of Asia. . .and if you dispute my right to the kingdom, stay and fight another battle for it; but do not run away. For wherever you may be, I intend to march against you." Accepting Darius' offer of friendship would have meant accepting him as an equal. And to Alexander this idea was as reprehensible as total surrender.

It was after his victory at Issus that Alexander told his staff he planned to invade Egypt. Possibly, as some historians believe, this had been his intention from the start. They maintain that Alexander's refusal to march east toward the heart of the Persian Empire indicates that he did not intend to capture it. But they forget that he was, above all, a general. And a general is as much concerned with what is behind him and around him as with what lies ahead. Alexander's wanderings in Asia were not aimless; he was continually securing bases in the rear and protecting his flanks. Obviously he could not consider plunging into central Persia until he had bases in Egypt.

Before he could invade Egypt, however, he had to capture Tyre. This city, in present-day Lebanon, was then the most powerful citadel on the eastern Mediterranean and the last big naval base left to the Persian fleet. When he prepared to besiege the city in January, 332, he called his intimate staff together. Arrian quotes him as having addressed them thus:

"Friends and allies, I see that an expedition to Egypt will not be safe for us, so long as the Persians retain command of the sea. Nor would it be safe, for various reasons, particularly the state of affairs in Greece, for us to pursue Darius, leaving in our rear this city of Tyre, of doubtful allegiance, and Egypt and Cyprus in the occupation of Persians. I am afraid that if we were to lead the army to Babylon in pursuit of Darius, the Persians might reconquer this seacoast and even carry the war into Greece with a still larger army. . ."

He went on to assure them that the conquest of Egypt would end all anxiety about the safety of Greece and thus permit the Macedonians "to undertake the expedition to Babylon with safety in regard to affairs at home." Possession of Egypt would also mean possession of the Persian ports along the seacoast of Phoenicia.

In Alexander's time, control of a sea depended on control of the majority of its ports. This was because of the frailty of warships of that day, which were swift, light galleys propelled mainly by oars. Galleys were seldom seaworthy in bad weather; thus their crews liked to stay near land, within sight of safe harbors where they could put in for repairs and supplies. A galley could not transport troops very far, and its principal combat mission—ramming an enemy head on—was suicidal by nature.

It will be recalled that Alexander ceased using his ships when he realized they could not outfight the larger Persian force. Since that time he had been virtually slamming doors in the face of the Persian fleet by sealing off its bases and havens. Although it could put to sea, it could not stay there indefinitely. His action had been highly effective in neutralizing Persian warships. Now if he could capture Tyre, only the ports in Egypt and Cyprus would remain available to the fleet.

Tyre, which had been built by the Phoenicians, consisted of two cities. One was on the mainland; the other lay behind a 150-foot wall on an impregnable, rocky island half a mile off the coast. Since its founding, some time before the fourteenth century B.C., the island fortress had withstood innumerable attacks and sieges. It had not even yielded to the thirteen-year siege of Babylonia's King Nebuchadnezzar in the sixth century.

Alexander took mainland Tyre readily, and then he set his chief engineer, Diades of Thessaly, to supervising the construction of a mole, or causeway, across the half a mile of sea to the island. The mole, which was to be two hundred feet wide, was an extraordinary engineering feat for the time and an innovation in warfare.

Mainland Tyre was leveled, and its rubble was carried to the construction site. Meanwhile, logs were dragged from the forests of Lebanon, and quarries were opened in the hills to supply stones for Diades' fabulous highway. Most of the troops, along with the hardiest inhabitants of the surrounding areas, were pressed into labor, and it is said that even Alexander himself carried stones on his back.

As construction of the mole inched ahead, the Tyrians sallied out of their island fortress in galleys and showered the workers with arrows. To keep these galleys at a respectful distance, two huge wooden towers were built and transported to the head of the mole. From their lower stories, catapults hurled missiles against the Tyrian galleys that came within range. From the top of the towers, which were as tall as the city's wall, missiles could be projected at soldiers defending the city.

One night, shielded by darkness, the wily Tyrians sent a ship laden with inflammable naphtha, her decks covered with wood shavings and sulphur, toward the unfinished mole. When the ship was near the towers, the crew ignited her and then swam off. Favored by wind, the flames enveloped the towers and destroyed them.

Undaunted, Alexander ordered new towers built and scoured Mediterranean ports for galleys which were needed desperately to screen construction of the causeway against attack. He collected 23 of them, and then good fortune favored him, as it did so often in his career. A fleet of some 80 Phoenician warships arrived on the scene; their crews had decided to throw in their lot with Alexander. Soon afterward, close to 120 more ships, from other new allies, joined the cause.

But the resourceful Tyrians were undismayed. They built their wall higher and thicker. They continued to raid the mole, and sallied out in their ships to strike at squadrons of Alexander's fleet. They improved their catapults and hurled a deadly new weapon—red-hot sand heated in huge cauldrons—which blinded and burned the Macedonians. Then, as the mole crept closer to the wall of Tyre, the defenders lowered fish nets and grappling hooks and deftly snatched up screaming Macedonians whom they tortured on top of the wall, in full view of helpless comrades.

By the time winter had passed and summer was approaching, Alexander may have come to question the wisdom of his causeway. Tyrian harassment had intensified into an everyday horror. And on more than one occasion the laborious work of many weeks was obliterated by the storm of a single night. But the work continued until at last the causeway was finished. Now Alexander assembled his siege engines and battering rams, and under a hail of sand and molten lead, he directed them against the wall of Tyre. Soon his worst fears were realized. Although the rams struck with great force, the Tyrian wall had been strengthened so stoutly that the huge, iron-headed rams were no more effective than men's fists would have been. The costly work of months ended in failure.

Alexander was discouraged but stubbornly refused to concede defeat. He mounted battering rams on some of his ships and probed the circumference of the island until a break could be made in the wall. But the Tyrians doggedly resisted any attempt to send troops through the breach.

Frustrated once again, Alexander decided to stage a general assault from three sides of the island. Squadrons of galleys, armed with catapults and loaded with archers, joined the ram ships to effect a pincerlike squeeze on the island fortress. When a large section of the wall was penetrated, ships equipped with boarding bridges were grounded on the island, and troops stormed into the city.

In the contest that followed, 8,000 Tyrians were slain. Two thousand others were marched down to the sea and hanged. The remaining 30,000, including women and children, were sold into slavery. Unable to forget the cruelties inflicted on the builders of the mole, Alexander vowed to show the defenders no mercy. He ordered the island destroyed—except the temples and the buildings that were essential to a Macedonian naval base. He was determined that the city should never rise again to thwart him. Long after his death, however, descendants of the conquered Tyrians straggled back to the rubble and built a new city that later prospered.

Tyre had fallen in July, 332, after a siege of seven months. Now Alexander had supremacy over the eastern Mediterranean. Thus, with little to fear for the security of his home base, he could concentrate entirely on land operations and on the conquest of Egypt.

VI

ALEXANDER THE GOD

Leaving ruined Tyre in his wake, Alexander marched south along the coastal road, probably expecting no further resistance until he invaded Egypt. He reached Gaza after traveling 150 miles and demanded that the city be surrendered immediately. To his surprise—and chagrin—Gaza's Persian governor would not oblige.

Gaza was a powerful fortress situated at the edge of the Egyptian desert and was set back from the Mediterranean on a high, steep mound. Batis, the governor, believed he could hold the city against Alexander until he was relieved by forces from Egypt or by the new army Darius was supposed to be raising far to the east.

Batis had good reason to feel confident, for Gaza

seemed impregnable—even Alexander's engineers said so. A lofty wall protected it on all sides, and the mound on which the city was built was so high that it was impossible to haul siege engines up to the wall. Yet the very impossibility of besieging this city convinced Alexander that it must be done. According to Arrian, he felt compelled to take Gaza because "the miracle of the achievement would strike terror into his enemies, while not to take it would be a blow to his prestige when noised about to the Greeks and Darius." Also, Alexander could not leave Gaza in Persian control, for it was on his line of communication.

So, with his chief engineer, Diades, Alexander devised an ingenious plan. He would build a countermound around the city—a ramp that would permit his siege engines to be drawn up on a level with the city's wall. This meant that once again his soldiers had to serve as laborers. The only material they would be able to use was what they had at hand—loose desert sand and soil. But these devoted and obedient fighters, men who had fashioned the causeway to Tyre, completed a workable ramp in an incredibly short period of time—and topped it off with a huge platform. Up the ramp and onto the platform the men dragged their catapults and battering rams, and then launched a massive assault. The wall stood. Alexander then had earth removed from beneath the wall to weaken its foundation.

After repeated attacks, sections of the great wall were at last beaten down, but the stubborn Gazans

hurled back their invaders. Finally, men of the Macedonian phalanx used scaling ladders to gain access
to the city. And in a violent hand-to-hand battle
among the debris of the once-impregnable wall, not
one defender escaped with his life.

Batis, though wounded severely, continued to fight
and resisted capture until he fainted from loss of blood
and fell into his enemies' arms. While Macedonian
soldiers plundered the fallen city, Alexander had the
unconscious Batis tied to a chariot and then dragged
him around the wall of Gaza. One who would try to
understand the character of Alexander cannot ignore
this scene in which the vengeful young conqueror,
urging his horses to go faster and faster, vented his
fury on a dying man who dared to resist him.

A few weeks after the fall of Gaza, Jerusalem submitted quietly. In November, 332, Alexander led his
army south from Gaza, and in seven days his troops
crossed 140 miles of Sinai desert to Pelusium, a citadel
on the Mediterranean that protected the eastern
approaches to Egypt. Alexander's siegecraft, shipped
by sea, arrived in advance, and there is every indication that Alexander planned to storm the ancient
fortress. But the fate of Tyre and Gaza had weakened
the resistance of the Persian authorities. They gave
up Pelusium at once, and within a few days surrendered Egypt to Alexander, handing over all the
gold in their treasury.

The quick capitulation of vast and wealthy Egypt
must have surprised the Macedonians. Yet nearly a
thousand years had passed since Egypt had been the

most powerful nation in the world. And since the coming of Darius, Egypt had been merely a part—the southwestern tip—of the Persian Empire. Most Egyptians loathed the Persian satraps; thus Alexander was looked on not as a conqueror but as a liberator, a champion of the oppressed.

For many years Egypt and Greece had enjoyed a close bond. Egypt had proved profitable to Greek traders who had settled there as early as the eighth century B.C. While Greek traders expanded their interests, Greek philosophers came to study in Egyptian schools, and Greek mercenary soldiers served Egyptian governments. Ultimately, Egyptian ideas became a more significant export to Greece than Egyptian grain. By the time Alexander marched into Egypt, as king of the Macedonians and captain-general of all Greece, the Egyptians and the Greeks had come to feel a strong spiritual kinship toward one another.

In all his Asian conquests Alexander had shown utmost respect for local religious customs. Now, in Egypt, he recognized the Egyptian gods as his gods. And his agents, hurrying in advance of his triumphal army, trumpeted the story Olympias had maintained to be true—that Alexander was the son of Zeus-Ammon. This was the foremost Egyptian god, whose mythical home was the oasis of Siwa, deep in the desert.

For centuries the Persian Great Kings had claimed to be pharaohs of Egypt by right of conquest. Now Alexander surpassed them in this respect; he claimed to be pharaoh by divine right—as the self-proclaimed son of Zeus-Ammon. This was an opportunity for which his mother had prepared him in childhood. And, as with every opportunity, he capitalized on it to every extent possible.

The reaction in Egypt to Alexander's assumption of deity was good. Even the powerful priesthood was delighted when assured that its position would remain unchanged. And Egypt's large Greek community, desiring increased trade with the homeland, was equally pleased that the new ruler was a Macedonian. Between the priests and the Greeks, public opinion favorable to Alexander spread through Egypt.

From Pelusium Alexander and his army took the desert highroad that led into the Nile valley near the site of modern Cairo. There his ships, which he had ordered to sail up the river, were waiting. Climbing aboard and crossing the Nile, he and his men were welcomed enthusiastically in the ancient Egyptian capital of Memphis.

After sacrificing to Apis, the sacred bull of Memphis, Alexander sailed along the western branch of the Nile to the Mediterranean coast. There on a wide strip of land between a lagoon and the sea, he proposed building a new seaport to be named Alexandria. Possibly this was his own idea; possibly it was suggested by Greek merchants who anticipated greatly increased trade between Egypt and other areas of the rapidly growing empire. Since the destruction of Tyre, a commercial center was needed on the eastern Mediterranean—a city which could serve as a cultural and administrative link between East and West.

Although Alexander founded at least nineteen cities in the course of his travels, none surpassed in grandeur the Egyptian port of Alexandria. The design of the city had been his own. Crouching over the black soil on which the city would be built, Alexander used flour to lay out a semi-circular plan. The details of the plan were later worked out by Dinocrates, the Macedonian architect who had been building a new temple of Artemis at Ephesus. An imaginative man, Dinocrates had delighted Alexander by proposing to carve the face of six-thousand-foot Mount Athos in Macedon into a gigantic likeness of Alexander standing waist-deep in the sea, supporting a city in one hand and a reservoir in the other. Actually, Dinocrates never had time to undertake that project, but in developing Alexander's plans for the new port city he gave his bold imagination full play.

Alexandria was to contain an *agora*, or forum, a university, a theater, a library, a gymnasium, courts of justice, and a temple to Poseidon, god of the sea. The city was to be surrounded by walls, and its streets, unlike the twisting roadways of other cities in that age, would run parallel and at right angles to a main thoroughfare, thus composing blocks. Though primarily a Macedonian colony, Alexandria was conceived of as a large cosmopolitan center with Egyptian, Greek, and Phoenician quarters.

Leaving the site of his proposed city, Alexander traveled some two hundred miles west along the desert seacoast to the village of Paraetonium. There he was met by ambassadors from Cyrene, the old and power-

This detail from a Pompeian floor mosaic is regarded as the definitive portrait of Alexander the Great. The mosaic was unearthed from a once lavish Pompeian villa known as the House of the Faun. It possibly depicts the Battle of Issus. It has been conjectured that the mosaic is a copy of a fourth century B.C. fresco by Philoxenos of Eretria, described in the histories of Pliny the Elder.

A third-fourth century B.C. bronze statue depicts Alexander taming his horse, Bucephalus. Plutarch wrote of Alexander's acquisition of Bucephalus from his father Philip II, who claimed the horse was impossible to train. Suspecting that the animal's nervous temperament was caused by a fear of its own shadow, Alexander kept Bucephalus's shadow behind its body, hidden from its view. After witnessing his son calm the wild horse, Philip II was said to have remarked, "O my son, look thee out a kingdom equal to and worthy of thyself, for Macedonia is too little for thee."

This third century B.C. bust of Alexander was found near Pergamon, Turkey. Today, he is revered as a kind of folk hero. There is little evidence of how he was perceived during his lifetime. In ancient historical texts his character varies from despotic insanity to heroic genius.

The construction of Alexandria, shown in a detail from a fifteenth century painting, began in 334 B.C. Several myths surround the founding of Alexandria, one of which tells of Alexander designing the original city plans by making a map with bits of grain. Diviners saw this as a sign of the city's future grain prosperity. During the Ptolemaic dynasty, Alexandria became a major grain supplier to Roman world.

The ancient Greek legend of the Gordian Knot is based on one, possibly more, oracles. According to legend, an oracle foretold to the people of Phyrgia that their future king would arrive in town on a wagon. When the peasant Gordius entered the city on an ox cart, the citizens believed that the prophecy had come true and made him their king. In gratitude, Gordius dedicated his cart to Zeus. He tied the cart with an intricate knot, the Gordian Knot. Another oracle, or perhaps the same one (the legend is vague on this point) claimed that whoever was able to untie the knot would rule Asia.

A fifteenth-century French book illustration shows Alexander the Great descending into the sea in a diving bell wearing his crown. According to legend, he used diving bells to clear the harbor of the ancient Phoenician city Tyre, 51 miles from modern day Beirut, Lebanon, before laying siege on the city in 332 B.C.

Ruins of the Bouleuterion, or assembly hall, in the ancient city of Priene in modern Turkey. Alexander stayed in Priene during his siege of Miletus, one of the many Ionian towns he took over after defeating the Persians in the Battle of Granicus.

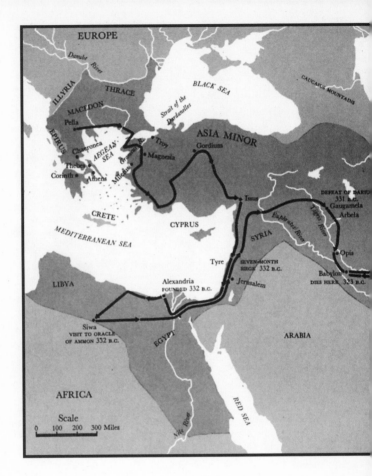

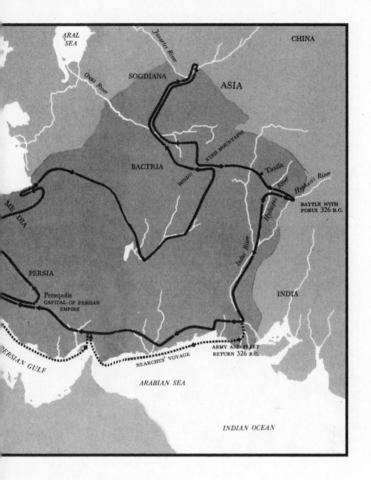

Map of Alexander's route of conquest.

The ruins of the Lycian tombs at the ancient Greek city of Xanthos, in southwest Turkey, from approximately the 4th century B.C. Ancient Lycians believed that the souls of their dead were carried away by birds, so they built their tombs on cliff tops. More than a thousand tombs, sarcophagi, and funerary monuments scattered throughout the Lycian towns of Xanthos, Patara, Myra and Phaselis suggest that funerary rites and the afterlife played a considerable role in ancient Lycian culture. Alexander conquered the Lycian towns in 334 B.C.

Alexander is portrayed as Heracles on a silver tetradrachme from around 300 B.C. Alexander's mother, Olympias, raised him believing he was a descendant of the Greek mythological heroes, Hercales and Achilles. She also claimed that Alexander's biological father was not Philip II but Zeus, who, in the form of a snake, impregnated her.

An elaborate floor mosaic found in a villa in Pompeii, composed of over two million tiles, portrays Alexander driving through the Persian line toward King Darius, in the Battle of Issus. Alexander's superior military stratagems allowed his greatly outnumbered forces to breach the Persian's front line, causing Darius and his troops to flee the battleground.

The family of King Darius at the feet of Alexander in a seventeenth century painting by Charles Le Brun. After being driven from the battlefield at Issus, King Darius fled the country, leaving his wife and children at Alexander's mercy. Alexander treated them with consideration and respect. Wanting to fuse Hellenistic and Persian cultures, Alexander supposedly encouraged and in some accounts, even bribed his soldiers to marry Persian women.

Alexander the Great enters the city of Babylon, Mesopotamia, 50 miles south of modern day Baghdad, Iraq, in an eighteenth century painting by Gaspare Diziani. Glad to be rid of Persian rule, the Babylonians peaceably surrendered to Alexander and his men. Alexander, taking precautions against what might be a trap, commanded his men to march into the city as if they were going into battle anyway.

A silver ten-drachma coin probably depicts Alexander in armor, holding in his right hand a spear and in his left hand a thunderbolt, which could signify either his deification or the legend that he was the son of Zeus. The coin dates to 324 B.C. After Alexander conquered India, he began issuing coins with his image.

The funeral procession of Alexander the Great depicted by Andre
Bauchant, a twentieth-century painter. In early June of 323 B.C.,
Alexander was in Babylon, planning another major military
campaign, historians conjecture, along the north African coast.
During his stay, at the palace of Nebuchadnezzar II, Alexander
contracted a fever and died within a few days.

ful Greek colony that dominated the Libyan tribes to the west of Egypt. Presenting such valuable gifts as three hundred horses and a crown of gold, the ambassadors turned over their vast territory to Alexander. He now held in his dominion the entire eastern end of the Mediterranean—all the way to the boundaries of the state of Carthage.

At this point one might have expected Alexander to turn east again, resuming his search for Darius. Instead, he set out to the south—across 180 miles of wind-blown Libyan desert to the oasis of Siwa to consult the oracle of Zeus-Ammon. So far as the Greeks were concerned, this oracle was almost as important as the oracle of Apollo at Delphi.

Many biographers believe that because of the strong and lasting influence of his mother, Alexander had harbored a belief that he actually was a god. They maintain that from the moment he set foot in Asia his ultimate goal had been to visit the oracle at Siwa and substantiate his immortality. This was probably not so. But since Alexander had come within a relatively short distance of one of the world's most renowned oracles, it is understandable that he succumbed to his superstitious nature and visited the shrine. Also, he may have had a military motive: by making the trek he would prove at last that the vast desert actually existed and could serve his purpose as a natural, protective boundary.

The march to Siwa would be dangerous, his advisers insisted. If he and his men should use up their water supply, they would experience great thirst for many days. And if a violent wind swept across the desert, they might be buried by the billowing, blowing sands. But Alexander would not be swayed from his mission. Plutarch points out that Alexander had developed a passion for overcoming hardships; "as if it were not enough to be always victorious in the field, unless places and seasons and nature herself submitted to him."

Nature and the weather did submit to him on this journey. Or perhaps, as Plutarch suggests, the gods were being extremely kind. First, there were plentiful rains, which relieved the fear of thirst and made the desert moist and firm to walk on. Then when the men became lost, "they were set right again by some ravens, which flew before them on their march and waited for them when they lingered and fell behind."

Alexander reached the shrine, finally, and according to Arrian, "surveyed the site with wonder." The high priest stepped forth and greeted him loudly as the son of Ammon—which could not be considered extraordinary, for he had come, after all, as pharaoh. And to Egyptians every pharaoh was a son of their chief god. Immediately Alexander asked if all those concerned with the murder of his father had been punished. In reply the oracle counseled him to speak with more respect, for no mortal could kill his true father, who was Ammon.

Soon after his visit to the oracle, Alexander began wearing the two ram's horns that were identified with Zeus-Ammon. He attached them to a band around his head so that they appeared to be growing from his blond hair, just above the ears. How strongly they impressed his Egyptian subjects is demonstrated by the fact that for centuries he was remembered as "the Two-Horned."

The more Alexander assumed the prerogatives of a god the firmer his position became with respect to the Egyptians. But if it was desirable for him to appear god like to his new subjects, it was highly undesirable for him to present himself as other than a mortal to the Macedonians. His godly aspect irked his countrymen. Even his close friend Philotas, who was Parmenio's son and captain of the Companions, was dismayed. In a letter quoted by Curtius, Philotas congratulated Alexander on his entrance into the ranks of the gods. And Philotas added wryly that he pitied those people who were ruled by a king who was more than a man. Later events reveal that Alexander never forgave Philotas this remark.

Alexander did not insist on being treated as a god. But he did not discourage this treatment whenever it was offered him. Being a god to some and a mortal to others was neither easy nor practical, and it became an acute psychological problem as well as a political dilemma with which he had to grapple. When Alexander let himself be considered a god, he ceased taking himself seriously as a man.

VII

PURSUIT OF DARIUS

When Alexander returned to captured Memphis, he set up a new government—taking care to appoint Egyptian officials to all the key posts. This was part of his own plan for administering conquered peoples, but it must have been rankling to his Macedonians, who thought they should have been given the opportunity to govern.

Word now reached Alexander that Darius was assembling a million men to fight him. The report was exaggerated, and Alexander must have known it, but he immediately gathered together an army. In the spring of 331, after organizing an occupying force to remain in Egypt, he set out to crush the Persians.

Moving north along the Mediterranean coast, he

turned inland at Tyre and marched through present-day Syria to the Euphrates. Hearing that Darius' army was to the east in the Tigris River valley, he pressed on three hundred miles more and finally reached the river north of modern Iraq. By late September the army was marching south along the eastern bank of the Tigris, skirmishing with squadrons of Persian cavalry that were keeping it under surveillance. Darius had established his base at Gaugamela, near the town of Arbela. Determined not to repeat his mistake at Issus by picking a narrow field, he had cleared a wide area as level as a parade ground, where his cavalry would have ample space in which to maneuver.

About seven miles from Gaugamela, Alexander rested his army again, this time in a well-entrenched position. One can imagine the state of mind of the women of Darius' family as they waited in the Macedonian camp. They too must have suffered greatly on the long march. Now they knew that if Alexander were defeated in the coming battle, they probably would be slain by the fleeing Macedonians. And if the Persians were defeated, Darius surely would be slain. By this time, Queen Statira had died—from exhaustion and the strain of worry.

Plutarch recounts that one of Statira's personal servants had escaped to Darius' camp and informed the Great King of her death. The grieving Darius was suspicious that Alexander might have been his wife's lover, but the servant had assured him that this was not so, praising Alexander's kindness and courtesy to the royal family. It can be assumed that Alexander was always prepared to extend similar courtesies to Darius himself—but only if the Great King would come personally to surrender and beg for amnesty. Otherwise the young conqueror was determined to destroy Darius and wipe out the entire Persian fighting force.

Arrian reports that Alexander's army numbered 40,000 infantry and 7,000 cavalry at this time. Darius' army was probably three or four times larger. It was a vast horde that included Bactrians, Indians, Persians, Parthians, Medes, Arabs, and Syrians. Among them, besides cavalry and columns of elephants, was a squadron of 200 four-horse chariots—to whose wheels sharp knives were attached. These vehicles were designed to operate against a line of tightly grouped soldiers, like a deadly mowing machine.

The night before the battle, Alexander reconnoitered the field of Gaugamela. With his commanders at his side, he observed the fires and torches from the huge Persian camp, which spread all over the plain. The sounds they heard issuing from that direction were "like the distant roaring of a vast ocean," says Plutarch.

Alexander's older generals, overwhelmed by the thought of facing a multitude such as Darius had brought together, urged Alexander to attack at night. In reply, he declared hotly, "I will not steal a victory," for he wanted nothing to detract from the great show of courage and tactical supremacy that would be his if he were able to rout the Persians. Also, he knew that battles fought at night seldom were decisive, and he intended that this battle should be—to establish him finally as the lord of Asia. In an eloquent speech to his men, he told them that this indeed would be their last great contest. Then, as before every engagement, he performed mysterious rites with his chief astrologer, Aristander—"sacrificing to the god Fear," says Plutarch.

As he emerged from his tent on the morning of the crucial battle, Alexander wore a tight-fitting coat and a breastpiece of thickly quilted linen which had been taken at Issus. His white-plumed iron helmet was so brightly polished that it shone like silver, and fitted to it was a collar set with precious stones. His sword, a gift from the king of the Citieans, hung from an elaborately worked belt given to him by the Rhodians.

Bucephalus was growing old now. So when Alexander was preparing for the battle, drawing up his troops and giving them directions, he spared Bucephalus and used another horse. But, says Plutarch, "when he was actually to fight, he sent for him again, and as soon as he was mounted, commenced the attack."

Gaugamela, sometimes called Arbela, was the most spectacular battle Alexander ever fought. In his traditional manner he took the initiative, but his tactics were different from those he had used at Issus and at the Granicus. First he moved toward the extreme left of the Persian ranks, drawing his enemies onto rough ground where their chariots would be useless. Darius tried to check this action with his cavalry and then sent his chariots thundering forward. But Alexander's skillful bowmen shot down the charioteers; the infantry opened ranks to let the careening chariots pass through, and the charge ended in failure. Now Alexander proceeded with his battle plan, which was to shatter the Persian left wing before the right wing could attempt to overwhelm his own weaker left commanded by Parmenio. At the same time Alexander did not forget that the chief target was the Persian center, where Darius had posted himself with his platoon of bodyguards.

As Alexander forced the Persian left flank to extend itself and become confused, he suddenly found the opening he had been seeking—a widening gap between his enemy's left and center. With the bristling spears of the heavy-infantry phalanxes as support, he and his Companions charged through the gap, wheeled around, and crashed into Darius' bodyguards from the rear.

In the hand-to-hand fight that followed, Darius, standing in his chariot, found himself at close range to Alexander. The Great King flung his spear at Alexander's head. He missed, and then according to Arrian, "when the Macedonian cavalry, commanded by Alexander himself, pressed on vigorously, thrusting themselves against the Persians and striking their faces with their spears, and when the Macedonian phalanx in dense array and bristling with long pikes had also made an attack upon them, all things together appeared full of terror to Darius, who had already long been in a state of fear." Leaping from his chariot, Darius vaulted onto a horse and fled from the field toward Arbela. His troops in the center, unnerved by his flight, began to scatter.

Alexander was prevented from pursuing Darius by the arrival of a messenger with a desperate plea from Parmenio. The Macedonian left wing, now to Alexander's rear in the scythelike sweep of battle, had been surrounded and was threatened with annihilation. Alexander was furious at having to quit the chase, but he swiftly led a body of troops to Parmenio's aid. In the final encounter of the battle, Hephaestion was wounded and sixty of Alexander's Companions were slain. Then the Persian resistance broke under the pressure of Alexander's mighty assault, and as word of Darius' flight spread, the entire Persian army withdrew.

Alexander now took up the pursuit of Darius. He rode half the night, not stopping until he reached Arbela. It was deserted; the Great King once again had vanished.

Eventually Alexander learned that about two thousand Greek mercenaries, accompanied by Persian and Bactrian cavalry and remnants of other units, had escaped with Darius along the road to Ecbatana in Media. Realizing that he could not overtake them, Alexander turned back, ending the chase. It was said that he never forgave Parmenio for having asked his aid at Gaugamela, thus keeping him from catching the Great King. Yet Parmenio's request seems to have been wholly justified. In his eagerness to destroy Darius, Alexander had permitted a wide gap in his own lines. If Parmenio's left wing had been overwhelmed, the battle at best would have ended inconclusively.

But it was a decisive victory for Alexander. Even though Darius had escaped with his life, his army was scattered, no longer of use to him. Accurate casualty figures on the battle do not exist; however, the significant fact about Gaugamela was that on its field the military strength of the Persian Empire was finally shattered.

From Arbela Alexander marched his army south 180 miles to Babylon, a winter capital of the Persian kings. If he had expected resistance from the Babylonians, he was surprised, for they poured out of their city to greet him with incense and garlands of flowers. Like the Egyptians, the Babylonians professed no love for the Persians; thus Alexander, their liberator, entered Babylon in triumph.

The tough Macedonians in the ranks were moved by the sight of their leader being welcomed so jubilantly, but they became disgruntled when Alexander refused to let them plunder Babylon. They did not go unrewarded, however. Alexander now possessed so much of the Great King's wealth that he could pay off his men handsomely. Curtius states that with their money "they wallowed in all the vices of this wicked city."

There is no indication that Alexander personally shared his troops' dissipations apart from his apparent tendency to drink more and more. As had become his habit after the rigors of a campaign, he occupied himself with religious rites. Babylon meant a new god as well as a new conquest to him. Bel, or Marduk, was the chief Babylonian god, and Alexander, surrounding himself with priests and magicians, worshiped him with conspicuous enthusiasm. In Arrian's words, "Whatever they directed him to do in regard to religious rites, he did."

As politically astute as his worship of the Babylonian gods was his appointment of a Persian viceroy to govern all of Babylonia. He gave this post to none other than Mazaeus, the general who had nearly crushed Parmenio's left wing at the battle of Gaugamela. The appointment must have delighted the Babylonians, but it probably added to the Macedonians' displeasure. Alexander knew, but they did not, that force alone would not be sufficient to weld the countries he had overwhelmed into one world power.

Alexander lingered only a month in Babylon, for he wanted to hasten on with the task of destroying Darius and absorbing the rest of the Persian Empire. And at about this time he was beginning to dream of a goal never before considered by a Westerner—the conquest of India.

From Babylon he marched his army 230 miles east to Susa, another of Darius' capitals. As in Babylon, the conquerors were greeted warmly, and Alexander retained the Persian satrap in office.

Although he vested himself with unlimited power, he was quick to give back a measure of authority to those he conquered. But if he seemed benign as a conqueror, he also seemed to enjoy indulging his royal prerogatives. Curtius and Diodorus tell a story about Alexander in Susa that was probably characteristic of him. When he sat down on the throne of

Darius, who was extraordinarily tall, he found that his feet did not touch the floor. So he asked that a low table standing nearby be pushed under his feet. As he settled his sandals on it, a slave of Darius' began to weep. Astonished, Alexander asked to know what was wrong, and the slave explained through his tears that he could not bear to see anyone's feet resting on the table from which Darius had eaten. Alexander apologized, saying that he would find another footrest. But one of his Companions urged him not to. It was a wonderfully good omen for him to put his feet on this table, the man said, for it indicated that soon Alexander would be trampling on Darius. Alexander, ever the believer in omens, forgot the sorrow of the Persian slave and ordered his friends to shove the table back under his feet.

In Susa a tremendous fortune in gold and silver passed into Alexander's hands. As was his custom, he distributed much of it among his troops and sent extravagant gifts to many parts of his growing empire, keeping little for himself. And at this time he assured the Persian royal family that their wanderings had ended. He established the aging Queen Mother Sisygambis in a splendid palace, along with her granddaughter, who was named after her mother, Statira.

Early in December, 331, Alexander led his army out of Susa toward Persepolis, the chief capital of Persia, some four hundred miles to the southeast. It was a perilous undertaking, for the route led over range after range of rugged mountains covered with deep winter snow. The march was as cruel as it was unnecessary, for it served no good military purposes. Alexander, revered as a god and near the pinnacle of his fame, seemed to be growing careless of life—his own and the lives of his men.

Halting before the last great mountain range that barred the way to Persepolis, he sent Parmenio ahead with the baggage train and the more heavily armed troops. Then with the heartiest of his Macedonians he stormed a Persian stronghold in a mountain pass called the Persian Gates. In a bitter fight in the sub-zero temperatures, the Macedonians slaughtered the enemy force that protected the pass, and marched swiftly out of the mountains.

Rejoining Parmenio, Alexander entered Persepolis before the huge Persian treasury could be removed. He told his men they could plunder all of the city except the palace, which he was planning to appropriate. After this, one of the most barbaric episodes in history took place. Seldom in his life did Alexander seem so debased as at Persepolis. By his own order, hundreds of citizens were rounded up and massacred. The Persians who escaped this slaughter did so only by leaping from the city walls or committing suicide in other ways. Apparently the bloodshed and looting continued uncontrolled for several days.

Parmenio, ever the counselor of moderation, begged Alexander to call a halt to the reign of terror. By destroying the city, he said, Alexander was demonstrating merely that he sought vengeance and did not intend to retain possession of Persia. But Parmenio no longer had much influence on Alexander's decisions. Soon, however, the troops exhausted themselves in bestiality, and Alexander set up his court in Darius' magnificent palace, which was famed throughout the East for its beautiful gardens and its splendid halls pillared with cedar wood.

The Macedonians were never quite the same after they began to enjoy the spoils of Persepolis. The wealth that became theirs was staggering. Alexander wrote his mother that five thousand camels and twenty thousand mules could scarcely have carried all the gold and silver and rich furnishings that had been seized in the capital and divided among his men. Plutarch says that Olympias wrote back a stern letter, cautioning her son to be more moderate in rewarding and honoring those who served him. "For now," she warned, "you make them all equal to kings, you give them power and the opportunity of making many friends of their own, and in the meantime you leave yourself destitute." Alexander continued to send her gifts—and wrote to her faithfully—but he refused to deny his men a share of the booty.

Alexander's Companions and chief officers had come from petty aristocracy, eking out a meager living from the soil of the Macedonian mountains. When they joined Alexander on his great adventure, they were seeking the spoils of war. But never had they imagined such luxury as they found in Persia. It overwhelmed them, and many of them did absurd things. One man sent a camel train all the way to Egypt to bring him a special powder to prevent his perspiring when he wrestled. Another insisted that even the nails in his boots be of pure silver. And Parmenio's son, Philotas, ordered the weaving of huge nets—twelve miles long—into which his beaters could drive the game he hunted. His mode of living became so excessive that even his spendthrift compatriots were scandalized.

Alexander, personally, continued to live a relatively simple life while lavishing his new wealth on his friends. Apparently his one dissipation was wine. In the evenings he would drink himself into a stupor—and then make bombastic speeches, gesturing grandiosely. But he soon had his fill of life in Persepolis. When he learned that Darius was trying to raise another army in Ecbatana, five hundred miles to the northwest, he made plans to march against the Great King once more.

Before setting out he gave a great banquet for his friends and officers and their women. As Plutarch describes it, the banquet became a brawl. At the height of the hubbub, Thais, the beautiful Athenian who had become the mistress of Alexander's general Ptolemy, staggered to her feet and made a speech. She said it would be sporting, and also a fitting climax to the irksome fatigues of following the army, if she were allowed to set fire to the Persian palace. This action, she declared, would do more to avenge the sufferings inflicted on the Greeks by the Persians than any battle, on land or sea.

Her request was received with cheers and applause. Everyone but Parmenio shouted approval. And Alexander expressed delight. With him in the lead, wearing a garland of flowers on his head, the soldiers and their women snatched up torches and danced through the halls of the palace, banging drums and blowing flutes as they lit the fires. Flames crept up the cedar pillars and enveloped the tapestries, and soon much of the palace was ablaze. By morning it was a smoldering ruin.

Plutarch, Curtius, and Diodorus believe that the burning of the palace resulted from drunken folly. But Arrian disagrees. He maintains that it was a deliberate act, approved by Alexander as a matter of policy, and intended to symbolize to the world the final degradation of the Persian Empire.

After wintering in Persepolis, Alexander and his men set out again in search of Darius. They reached Ecbatana late in the spring of 330 and found that the Persian monarch and a few thousand of his troops had departed, heading now toward the province of Bactria, which was ruled by a Persian viceroy named Bessus. At Rhagae, near modern Tehran, Alexander learned that Bessus had imprisoned Darius and declared himself the new Great King.

Now, in search of a new enemy, Alexander hastened his march northeast. Even his best troops were beginning to fall by the wayside as he moved nearer to what is today the Russian border. Soon, overcome by weariness and thirst, the men who remained were ready to give up. They might have died there if Alexander had not spurred them on with another display of his stamina and self-denial.

According to Plutarch, some Macedonians from the

ranks set out one day determined to find water for the children who were with them on the march. After a long and discouraging search, they were successful—and joyfully returned to camp. There they saw Alexander almost choked with thirst, and filling a helmet, they offered the water to him instead. Plutarch says that Alexander "took the helmet into his hands, and looking round about, when he saw all those who were near him stretching their heads out and looking earnestly after the drink, he returned it again with thanks without tasting a drop of it. 'For,' said he, 'if I alone drink, the rest will be out of heart.' The soldiers no sooner took notice of his temperance and magnanimity upon this occasion but they one and all cried out to him to lead them forward boldly, and began whipping on their horses." Once again, by setting an example for his men, he had won their confidence and ignited their enthusiasm. The Macedonians soon were back on the march.

At some unidentified spot in the desert south of the Caspian Sea, they found Darius, but Bessus was nowhere in sight. Before fleeing, Bessus and some of his men had stabbed the Great King with their spears and had flung him into a cart. One of the Companions found Darius, near death, and gave him water. Plutarch says that Darius praised Alexander for his kindness to the royal family and then died before Alexander himself arrived on the scene. Expressing deep sorrow over the way Darius had met his end, Alexander covered the Great King with his own purple cloak.

Darius' body was sent back to Persepolis where it received a splendid funeral and was placed in the royal tomb along with past Persian monarchs. Now that Darius was dead, Alexander was Great King by right of conquest. But Bessus continued to claim this title. And he continued to go free, unpunished, as he headed for Bactria, almost a thousand miles away. There would be no peace in Persia or in Alexander's mind until he had captured Bessus and all resistance to his rule had ended.

VIII

THE NEW GREAT KING

The Macedonians were tired of war. They had been away from home four and a half years and had marched more than seven thousand miles. They had fought innumerable battles and skirmishes, endured every conceivable hardship, grown rich, become homesick—yet they were being asked to march again, farther from home than ever.

The army had changed considerably since the day it paraded out of Pella in straight, even columns. On the move now it looked like a caravan, a colony of emigrants, and its encampments resembled not so much military bases as sprawling tent cities. Often one would have had difficulty locating the soldiers among all the shopkeepers, vintners, priests, slaves, actors, musicians, wives, and children who accompanied the expedition.

When the troops left Pella, their confidence in Alexander was almost boundless. Now there was considerable grumbling about the twenty-six-year-old conqueror. His men had come to realize that he might never be content achieving one goal without wanting to press on toward another. They could hardly help wondering what his ultimate plans were. And they wondered too at his actions, for he had begun to seem more like a Persian than a Macedonian. He even wore Persian clothes, on occasion. Was he indeed succumbing to the perfumed intoxication of life in Asia? Was he turning himself into an Oriental potentate? The Macedonians, accustomed to settling their differences immediately and with violence, talked among themselves and grumbled. But for the time being they continued to follow their leader.

Alexander was aware of the grumbling, but he tried as much as possible to ignore it. When he could not, he praised his men and cajoled them or bribed them with bonuses and promises of plunder. He believed in earnest that his destiny was to overcome all opposition, and it hardly mattered if this opposition came from his newly conquered subjects or from the men who were his followers.

He needed the wholehearted support of his army, now more than ever, for the task immediately before him was to force the surrender of those followers of Darius who still held out against him. And he would also have to subdue the rebellious tribes that had always denied the authority of Darius and were now refusing to recognize Alexander as their leader. In blasting winds and under burning sun, through desolate mountains and across broad deserts, Alexander marched—working to secure the north-eastern frontiers of his empire as methodically as he had secured its southwestern frontiers in Egypt.

After giving his army a long rest at Zadrakarta, near the southeastern shores of the Caspian Sea, he set out on a 550-mile march across the northern part of present-day Iran. Everywhere he went his purpose was to obtain the submission of Darius' satraps, and he put to death any man who had betrayed Darius and become allied with Bessus. Evidently he saw nothing wrong in defending the rule of the man who so recently had been his mortal enemy. He recognized that in becoming the avenger and protector of the Persian royal family he appeared to hold the divine right of succession, while Bessus was only a pretender to the throne.

Perhaps Alexander did regard himself now, first and foremost, as the Great King of the Persian Empire. Certainly he revered this title more than the others to which he had laid claim. But he did not ascend to this pinnacle unaided, and he knew he could not properly govern his empire without assistance. However, he did not trust his Macedonian followers; even the most loyal of them no longer had his complete confidence. He valued their indomitable spirit in battle, but he was aware that they could be irresponsible in peacetime. And now their growing discontent was beginning to annoy him. Was he not, after all, their Great King?

Alexander's doubt about the loyalty of some of his men was expressed dramatically near the end of the year 330 when the army had reached Drangiana, a province in what is now western Afghanistan. There the Macedonians' discontent with the long campaign erupted in an apparent plot against Alexander's life.

Parmenio's son, Philotas, had known of the plot, but for reasons that are still unknown, did not inform Alexander. Learning of this, Alexander concluded that Philotas had been one of the plotters and had him arrested. The Macedonians were stunned when Alexander called them together to announce, with much emotion, the arrest of his old friend whose father was then on garrison duty in Ecbatana. He produced a letter which he said contained evidence that incriminated Philotas. Then he charged that Philotas had been claiming—for himself and his father—the credit for all of Alexander's victories. Finally he recalled how Philotas had sneered at the revelation that Alexander was a god.

Philotas spoke eloquently in his own defense, insisting that he never believed a plot against Alexander existed, and that what he had heard, but not reported, he had considered merely drunken talk. Apparently Philotas convinced most of his listeners that there was no case against him, but that night he was tortured while Alexander listened behind a curtain. At last, after being lashed with whips and scorched with red-hot coals, he screamed a confession that implicated his father and a number of Macedoni-an soldiers.

When Philotas was carried before the troops the next morning and was forced to repeat the confession, his comrades stoned him and stabbed him to death with their javelins. Then they declared that the soldiers he had implicated were also guilty, and they killed them all summarily.

Alexander immediately dispatched an officer named Polydamas to kill Parmenio. Traveling by camel, Polydamas completed the nine-hundred-mile journey to Ecbatana in eleven days. Finding Parmenio in his garden, Polydamas said that he had a letter from Alexander. As Parmenio took the scroll in his hands, Polydamas ran him through the heart with a sword. He brought Parmenio's severed head to Alexander as proof that the old man indeed was dead.

This chronicle of horrors was typical of what was then called justice—a ritual that ran its course from suspicion and arrest to a trial supported by circumstantial evidence, a confession wrung by torture, and death. Parmenio's execution may seem to have been outright murder, but an old Macedonian law decreed that relatives of conspirators against the throne must also die.

It is difficult to believe that a man of Parmenio's character would participate in a plot against his leader's life. So far as is known he had no personal ambitions beyond serving his country, and he had been consistently loyal—even though he felt that Alexander went too far in emulating Persian customs. It is likely that Philotas implicated his father out of desperation, hoping to spare himself further torture.

Alexander may have realized this and could have waived the law in Parmenio's case, for he did owe much of his success to the general's wisdom and counsel. But he knew also that Parmenio would become his sworn enemy upon learning how Philotas had died. Nor could Alexander risk bringing Parmenio to trial, for the old man was so highly regarded that powerful elements in the army would probably side with him. And perhaps Alexander, ever the tactician, decided that by letting Parmenio pay the penalty of the law, he would break any Macedonian opposition to his rule once and for all.

The purge of the plotters did not end dissension in the Macedonian ranks, but it did cause many of Alexander's friends to regard him with terror. All of them followed, however, as he turned north in search of Bessus.

In the spring of 329, with customary impatience, Alexander set out to cross the towering Hindu Kush mountain range before its snows had melted. His men suffered woefully, and many froze to death before they completed the crossing and reeled down into the valleys.

Beyond the Oxus River, Alexander learned that Bessus, like Darius before him, had been imprisoned by one of his chief officers. The Macedonian cavalry finally caught up with Bessus in a tiny village where he had been abandoned. Alexander reacted with wanton cruelty when Bessus was turned over to him.

The former Persian viceroy was stripped naked and whipped until he was nearly dead. Then he was sent to the Bactrian capital of Zariaspa, where his nose and ears were cut off, and finally to Ecbatana, where he was sentenced to death after a mock trial. His hands and feet were lashed to saplings that had been bent to the ground. When the saplings were released—and flew upward—Bessus' body was ripped in half.

Now Alexander announced his intention of marching even farther north to the shadowy borders of his empire. Almost at once the Greek cavalry units that had served under Parmenio rebelled, and Alexander was forced to send them home. He considered the idea of ending his march at this point, for in so remote a locale he could not fill his depleted ranks with Macedonian or Greek replacements. Instead, he took a chance and recruited a body of Persian soldiers as reinforcements. They were barbarians and he was loath to trust them. But the compelling urge for survival forced him to do so—no matter how extraordinary it seemed then. Actually, the Persian troops were invaluable to Alexander; they were well trained for the sneak attacks and treacherous guerrilla warfare that awaited Alexander in the mountains of Bactria.

From the Oxus, Alexander marched more than three hundred miles north to Maracanda, which is now Samarkand in Uzbekistan. Then, continuing two hundred miles farther northeast, he reached the Syr Darya River, which was then called the Jaxartes. This river marked the northeastern boundary of the Persian Empire, and Alexander may have thought the river was part of a great sea that encircled the earth. He was surprised when emissaries came to him from northern regions where he was certain only water existed. Each of these ambassadors sought him as an ally in wars against peoples he had never heard of.

But Alexander was having enough troubles of his own without adopting those of strangers. At times he must have thought his new domain was an empire in name only. For the fierce peoples of the northeastern frontiers resented him bitterly—just as they had always resented an overlord, be he Darius or any other ruler. Their rebellious spirit was like an uncontrollable fire; when Alexander stamped it out in one place, it blazed up in another.

Across the desolate uplands and arid plains of present day Afghanistan, Uzbekistan and Turkmenistan, he marched and countermarched. And his army bathed itself in the blood of rebellious peoples. Alexander's method of putting down insurrections was brutal and not so effective as he wished it to be. When a viceroy betrayed him, he would seize perhaps half a dozen towns in the province, murder the men, and sell the women and children into slavery. Then he would repopulate the towns by bringing in settlers from neighboring regions in the hope of creating new allies.

In the fall of 328 Alexander appointed his old friend Cleitus to be viceroy of Bactria and Sogdiana. Cleitus was the man who had saved Alexander's life in the battle at the Granicus. Since Philotas' death he had shared with Hephaestion the command of the Companions. Alexander held a banquet to honor Cleitus on the occasion of his new appointment, and the festivities quickly turned into a scene of violence and tragedy.

All the Macedonians, as was their habit, became so drunk as to be beyond understanding—but not misunderstanding. Cleitus heard Parmenio's name being mentioned and apparently decided that Alexander was deriding the achievements of the murdered general. Cleitus had been Philotas' principal lieutenant, and he remained intensely loyal to the memory of the warrior father and son. Angrily he began to taunt Alexander for his Persian manners, his pretense of being a god, and according to Plutarch, rebuked him for disowning his father and ignoring the fact that it was "by the expense of Macedonian blood. . .that you are now raised to such a height."

Alexander, fully as drunk as Cleitus and unable to suppress his anger, snatched up a spear from one of the soldiers and ran his old friend through the heart. Alexander's immediate remorse was so great, says Plutarch, that he then tried to drive the spear into his own throat and would have done so "if the guards had not held his hands and by main force carried him away into his chamber, where all that night and the next day he wept bitterly."

By this time a pattern of behavior was emerging in Alexander. To offset the daily tensions of command and battle he sought release by drinking heavily, and the more he drank the more bombastic he became. He rejected criticism when he was sober and responded to it with violence when drunk. Usually his violence was followed by remorse—which did not last very long.

After the murder of Cleitus, the Companions sent in the chief philosophers of Alexander's retinue to console him. The first was an austere man named Callisthenes, who was a nephew of Aristotle. He used "moral language," says Plutarch, "and gentle and soothing means," but Alexander would not listen to him. The second man, Anaxarchus, cried out abruptly the moment he entered, "Is this the Alexander whom the whole world looks to, lying here weeping like a slave for fear of the censure and reproach of men?" He scorned Alexander's grief, insisting that a king could do no wrong and that Alexander had acted justly, according to the will of the gods. This cheered Alexander considerably. He decided that he had probably angered the god of wine, Dionysus, by destroying Thebes, seat of Dionysian worship—and concluded that the avenging Dionysus, rather than he personally, was to blame for the death of poor Cleitus. He made elaborate sacrifices to the god and then tried to forget the whole unfortunate incident.

Callisthenes and Anaxarchus had other occasions to oppose each other with respect to Alexander's actions. Each man enjoyed a position of prominence in the Great King's retinue, but they were remarkably dissimilar men. Callisthenes was moral and unyielding, schooled in cold Aristotelian logic. Anaxarchus was a shrewd flatterer who constantly sought his sovereign's favor. He pleased Alexander immensely by assuring him that he was right to demand obeisance of everyone in the Persian manner. But Callisthenes argued that the Greeks and the Macedonians should not have to kneel before their king and press their foreheads to the floor.

Needless to say, Callisthenes' viewpoint was popular with the Macedonians who were annoyed by Alexander's new notion that old friends must pay him such homage. When an alleged plot by Macedonian pages to murder Alexander was uncovered, one page launched an impassioned and bitter harangue against the Great King. He claimed that his inspiration had come from Callisthenes, whom he called the defender of Greek liberty.

Although Callisthenes knew nothing of the plot, the page's statement finished him. The fact that he was related to Aristotle did not temper Alexander's wrath, for the Great King had recently developed a dislike for his old tutor. Arrian says that Callisthenes was tortured and hanged. But other sources indicate that Alexander had him imprisoned and that he died of illness while awaiting trial.

In dealing so ruthlessly with opposition, and in demanding obeisance of everyone in his court, Alexander was now acting like a true Oriental potentate. It was a role he seems to have enjoyed, and at the same time it was one he believed essential to retaining the powers of a Great King. For how could he rightfully demand obeisance of his Eastern subjects while excusing Westerners from the practice?

Early in 327, as Alexander completed his plans to

invade India, he was exasperated to learn of the revolt of a prince of the province of Sogdiana. This prince was Oxyartes, and he carried out his defense strategy from a mountain fortress called the Sogdian Rock. Alexander wasted no time in moving north across the Oxus, and in an extraordinary feat of rock climbing he began a siege of the enemy stronghold. In one of the first actions of the campaign he captured Oxyartes' daughter, Roxana, who was described by historical authorities as one of the most beautiful women in the empire. Soon afterward Oxyartes surrendered, and no doubt he was astonished at how well Alexander treated him. He must have been even more astonished when he learned that Alexander had married his daughter.

Very possibly Alexander had a deep love for Roxana. If so, it is curious that she is not mentioned again by historians until four years after her marriage. But, alas for romance, there is no indication that Alexander ever cared for any woman other than his mother, Olympias. Perhaps his marriage was only a political union, for Alexander then placed his new father-in-law in charge of the troublesome Bactrian and Sogdian provinces. At last, under Oxyartes' administration, peace came to the northeastern frontier.

Now Alexander turned once again toward the rising sun, making clear his plan to advance beyond the Indus River, which was in theory the easternmost boundary of his empire. Before the new campaign began, he received a visit from the ruler of Taxila, which was between the Indus and Hydaspes rivers in present-day Pakistan. This ruler, who called himself Taxiles, asked Alexander to join him in a war against King Porus, who ruled a land that lay east of the Hydaspes—and Alexander agreed. Thus the march into India began.

Since the time he first came to power in the kingdom of Macedon, Alexander had been discovering that the world was bigger and more complex than even the wise Aristotle had imagined. Yet so far as can be determined, Alexander's eastward push was not motivated solely by a desire to subjugate strange peoples or by a thirst for world conquest. It is more likely that he led his troops into India because that rich land had once been part of Darius' empire. And only by subjugating India could he call his conquest of the Persian Empire complete and secure his claim to be the new Great King.

IX

ANOTHER WORLD TO CONQUER

In midsummer of 327 Alexander struck his great camp, which was near modern Kabul, capital of Afghanistan, and marched toward India. When he approached the Khyber Pass, he divided his army, which then numbered approximately forty thousand men. He sent one part of it through the pass under Hephaestion's leadership, and led the rest himself by a more difficult route to the north.

The movement of his troops was slow, and soon Alexander realized why. Their advance was hindered not only by the terrain but also by the staggering weight of the booty they had with them. At dawn one day, when all the freight was loaded, Alexander set fire to his own baggage wagon and then commanded that his soldiers' wagons be burned too. Surprisingly few men protested this action. Plutarch says that "most of the soldiers, as if they had been inspired, uttering loud outcries and warlike shoutings, supplied one another with what was absolutely necessary and burnt and destroyed all that was superfluous."

With their load thus lightened, the men were free to move on more easily—and to engage in some of the most difficult fighting of their lives. Nearly every mile of their progress was contested by fierce mountain warriors. It was not until early spring of 326 that Alexander at last rejoined Hephaestion and their reunited forces crossed the Indus into friendly Taxila.

A man who enjoyed combat less than Alexander might have become discouraged by this time. For having marched more than nine thousand miles up and down his empire, having lost many of his old friends and grown suspicious of others, he had found that each new victory led only to other battles. Now, in India, he faced hordes of well-organized and hot-tempered tribesmen who refused to recognize him as Alexander the Great, lord of Asia.

Nor was this resistance his only worry, for the morale of his Greek and Macedonian veterans was beginning to sag once again. The men were exhausted; they had already crossed the Indus into a kingdom which they were forbidden to plunder. And now Alexander was proposing to lead them across still another river—the Hydaspes, later called the

Jhelum—against a force more powerful than any they had faced since the battle of Gaugamela.

King Porus, who ruled the land beyond the Hydaspes, was a giant of a man, the bravest and most capable general Alexander would ever fight. His infantry is reported variously to have numbered between 20,000 and 50,000 men. And his 4,000-man cavalry was reinforced by chariots and about 200 elephants as well. These elephants served as his most potent arm of defense, for horses were terrified of the huge, lumbering creatures. In battle, Porus wisely perched his own huge frame on an elephant's back to make himself safe from the crushing charge of Alexander's mounted Companions.

To discourage Alexander from attempting to cross the Hydaspes, Porus ordered elephant-mounted troops to patrol the river's east bank near the fording place Alexander was expected to use. Alexander knew his horses would be useless here, for the moment they spied Porus' elephants they would shy in panic and become unmanageable. The only way Alexander could get a body of troops across the river was by deception—and surprise.

He had a flotilla of boats brought from the Indus and then made elaborate and very obvious preparations to stage a crossing. To keep Porus constantly on the move, he made numerous threats to cross the river at other points. After a time Porus ceased responding to these feints; he concluded that Alexander had no real intention of crossing until after the rainy season had passed.

Once assured that his deception was successful, Alexander took a select group of five thousand cavalry and more than six thousand infantry eighteen miles upriver from the ford. At night, and on rafts they had made from hides, these troops stealthily negotiated the river. Meanwhile, Alexander's main army remained alert and noisily present on the western side of the ford.

Shortly after daybreak the following morning, word reached Porus that a landing had been made. He dispatched a large reconnoitering force of cavalry to drive Alexander back, but Alexander scattered it quickly. Then, after leaving behind a small force of elephants and foot-soldiers to cover the river ford, Porus formed the main body of his army into a formidable array to meet Alexander's attack. In the center he placed his elephants, about a hundred feet apart, with the infantry massed behind them. His cavalry, reinforced by horse-drawn chariots, was aligned in depth on either wing.

Alexander did not dare launch a frontal attack. He knew his cavalry would be ineffective against Porus' widely deployed elephants. Actually his only hope for victory lay in using his infantry to wipe out Porus' elephant-mounted troops. And the only way he could possibly do this was by first overcoming the Indian cavalry with his own horsemen.

Alexander's cavalry was stronger and greater in number than Porus', but he could exploit this superiority only by drawing the Indian cavalry out of range of the elephants' protection. Everything depended on

Porus' responding precisely as Alexander anticipated. Never had the young King gambled against such heavy odds.

First he sent his horse archers against the cavalry on the Indian left flank. He followed up this thrust with an incisive attack by the Companions. Then Porus did just what Alexander had hoped. Seeing that the major blow was being administered to his left-wing cavalry, Porus swung his right wing around to support it.

Alexander's success in this battle was due in no small measure to superb timing as well as careful planning. Communication between commanders during the frenzied peak of battle was almost out of the question. But they knew exactly what they must do; Alexander had schooled them well. Thus when the strengthened Indian left wing advanced forward of Porus' elephants and infantry, the remainder of Alexander's horsemen almost instinctively galloped into action. Under the command of a general named Coenus, the horsemen poured out of the Macedonian left flank, made a wide lateral movement, and charged the Indian cavalry on its freshly exposed right side. Now Porus' two cavalry wings had to fight as one. And now they were being forced to fight Alexander's cavalry on two defensive fronts, facing opposite directions. To counteract this stunning maneuver, which had successfully cornered his horsemen, Porus drove his elephants to the left. This was, once again, exactly the reaction Alexander had hoped for. By shifting his elephants, Porus had exposed his right-wing infantry.

Now nothing stood in the way of a massive assault by the Macedonian heavy infantry, and it crashed into its more vulnerable opposition with an impact like a clap of thunder.

Almost at once the resistance crumbled, and the Indian infantrymen were driven back into the ranks of the elephants "as to a friendly wall for refuge," says Arrian. Alexander's infantry continued its attack and inevitably came face to face with the Indian elephants. Fearlessly the Macedonians advanced, and soon their ready bowmen were picking off the elephant drivers one by one. Left without guidance, the great beasts backed away from the shouting, shield-clashing Macedonians—in Arrian's words, "facing the foe like ships backing water and merely uttering a shrill piping sound."

Now Alexander prepared for the final surprise of this brilliantly fought battle, a knockout blow by his mounted Companions. Relentlessly they charged across the battlefield and poured into the heart of the Indian army.

Soon the Indian troops were in chaos, with frightened men running in all directions. Riderless, and wild with pain and fright, the trumpeting elephants trampled among them, while Alexander's infantry and cavalry hacked at them from all sides. Meanwhile, the Indians protecting the river ford had been driven away, and the bulk of Alexander's army poured across the Hydaspes. Streaming onto the battlefield, the fresh troops pursued the fleeing Indians.

In this eight-hour battle, Porus probably lost about

twelve thousand men, while Alexander's losses were little more than a thousand. Porus himself, though wounded, was one of the last to fight his way off the field. Sitting atop his lurching elephant, he hurled spears at Alexander's Taxilian allies, who begged him to surrender. When Porus finally pitched to the ground, weakened from the loss of blood, Alexander galloped up to him and through an interpreter asked how he expected to be treated. Porus, drawing himself up to his full seven feet, replied calmly and with dignity, "Like a king."

Never had Alexander been so won over by a foe. He made Porus his ally and eventually his friend, and to the disgust of the Macedonians and Greeks, he even forbade any looting of Porus' kingdom. Alexander's veterans seem to have been completely baffled by their leader's conduct. They had won a great battle only to find that when the dust on the battlefield had settled, the defeated enemy ruler remained in power while they personally were denied the spoils they had earned by their valor. What, they must have asked among themselves, did Alexander have in mind?

Reliable sources suggest that Alexander had little in mind at this point except the urge to continue his quest for military glory. He had advanced so far that his communications with the West were almost nonexistent. He appeared now to be more interested in extending his empire than in governing it. Certainly he enjoyed performing the role of Persia's Great King, but he was stimulated more by battle than by tending to affairs of state.

Moving eastward, he founded more cities—including one named after his horse Bucephalus, who had died of exhaustion during the battle of the Hydaspes. The cities did not endure long, however, for Alexander's men did not wish to remain on garrison duty in this strange land.

The kind of fighting they were called upon to do now was totally new to them. Fever and illness, instead of armed warriors, were their enemies. Added to this harassment was extreme heat succeeded by torrential, steaming rain. For seventy days, says Diodorus, the men slogged through a steady downpour. Their clothing was in rags, their armor rusted, and their weapons were dulled from carelessness and disuse. Apparently it was late summer when they came to the Hyphasis River, now called the Beas, which flows down from the Himalayas. They had zigzagged nearly 1,000 miles from the Indus and were about 250 miles northwest of modern Delhi.

When the rains stopped, Alexander could see the snowcapped peaks of the Himalayas gleaming in the distance. He may have thought that these mountains surely marked the end of the world. Soon, however, reports began coming to him from beyond the Hyphasis. Over there, he was told, lay the vast realm of a rajah, or king, who commanded an army of a quarter of a million men and thousands of elephants. And not a week's march away, he learned, there flowed a mighty river called the Ganges.

Alexander was not the only one to hear reports of what lay beyond the Hyphasis. Rumors began circulating among his troops—stories of enormous elephant armies, of warriors of extraordinary height and fierceness—and these rumors, magnified by the men's weariness and their fear of the unknown, caused the Macedonian morale to collapse. Some of the men declared openly that they would not go another step farther. Learning of this, Alexander called his officers together and addressed them in words quoted here in part from Arrian:

"Do you shrink from adding the Hyphasis and the land beyond this river to your empire of Macedon?. . .I, for my part, think that to a brave man there is no end to labors except the labors themselves, provided that they lead to glorious achievements. But if any of you wants to hear what will be the end of this warfare of ours, let him know that the distance still remaining before we reach the river Ganges and the Sea of the East is not great. And I tell you that the Hyrcanian Sea [Caspian Sea] will then be found to be united with that sea, because the great outer ocean encircles the whole earth.

"I will prove to you that the Indian Gulf flows into the Persian Gulf on the one hand and into the Hyrcanian Sea on the other. From the Persian Gulf our expeditionary force will sail round to Libya until we reach the Pillars of Heracles [Strait of Gibraltar]. All Africa and Asia will then belong to us, and the limits of our empire in these directions will be those which the gods have fixed as the limits of the earth."

Obviously Alexander was not speaking now as a god, as the son of Ammon, or as an Oriental potentate demanding obeisance of his subjects. Once more he was Alexander of Macedon, general of the army, good companion of his men. Always in past moments of crisis he had been able to incite his officers to ecstatic agreement by his eloquent and impassioned oratory. But now, beside the river that flowed toward a mysterious sea, with sunlight reflecting on distant mountains, his men stood silent with downcast heads.

Speak! Alexander commanded them. But there was only silence, and tears welled in the eyes of their weary, battle-scarred faces. Finally one man stepped forward—slowly and reluctantly. He was Coenus, a veteran who had borne the hardships of all the campaigns and had risen from obscurity to a position of command at the battle of the Hydaspes.

One can imagine that Coenus spoke haltingly at first. But gradually, as Arrian quotes him, his words flowed with an eloquence equal to Alexander's.

After recounting the memorable experiences Alexander and his men shared, Coenus cried, "Return, Alexander! Return to your own country, see your mother, and carry to the home of your ancestors the story of these victories so many and so great. Then, if you so desire, start afresh on a new expedition. . .Self-control, Alexander, in the midst of success is the noblest of all virtues!"

The officers who had affronted Alexander with their silence after he spoke now burst into cheers. And Alexander, turning on his heel, strode into his tent. For three days he remained there, speaking to no one. Never had his rage been so great. And never had he felt so much alone. Not a man would accompany him farther. That thought must have stung him repeatedly in the tumult of his emotions.

There beside the Hyphasis he may have glimpsed the irony of his success. He probably recognized that he had advanced so far and become so famous mainly because of his extraordinary ability to inspire others to follow him. Now, at the peak of his success, that ability had apparently run its course. Though he was angry and hurt, Alexander was realistic enough to realize that he could not afford to have his army desert him, for he could not go on alone.

On the third day of his troubled isolation, he summoned his seers and soothsayers to his tent and asked to know the omens for crossing the Hyphasis. The soothsayers were wise men, and politic too, and they knew how to save face for him. After performing solemn rites they reported that the gods did not wish him to cross the river.

Very well, Alexander said finally, he would turn back.

X

DEATH OF A MAN

To mark the farthest point of his march into India, Alexander had twelve towering altars erected, one for each of the gods of Olympus. Then, after his men had offered sacrifices and engaged in gymnastics and cavalry contests, he turned them away from the Hyphasis River and led them south. The men had won their point, but it was Alexander who chose their homeward route—and the path he picked was strange, indirect, and perilous.

By November, 326, he had returned to the Hydaspes and assembled a fleet of nearly a thousand small boats. He floated his army down that river and then down the Chenab River that joined it. He never ceased playing the role of conqueror, even on this final voyage. During the siege of one stoutly defended city, he leaped into battle from the city's walls with only three followers to protect him. Before he could be rescued he was wounded severely and for several days lay close to death. Meanwhile, word spread through camp that he had been killed, and his men became terrified. Although still angry at having been brought so far from home, they were certain that Alexander was the only one who could lead them back safely.

When Alexander learned that his death was being rumored, he had his attendants carry him to the river. There he was placed aboard a ship that was rowed along shore so his men could see that he was still alive. The wound had not been fatal, but indirectly, because it left him weakened, the injury was to cost him his life.

It was probably not until early spring, 325 B.C., that Alexander was recovered sufficiently to continue his voyage. Drifting down the Chenab, his ships reached the confluence with the Indus, and still they proceeded southward. Despite a promise to turn west into Persia, Alexander was determined to follow the Indus to its conclusion. When he finally sighted the Arabian Sea, beyond the mouth of the river, his joy was uncontained; he assumed he had reached the southern limit of the inhabited world.

His men did not share this joy, however. It was summer by then. Nearly a year had passed since they had turned back from the Hyphasis, but they were as far from home as before. And the sullen, gray ocean, which to them represented the end of the earth, filled them with fear.

Now they begged Alexander to resume the journey homeward, and he agreed. But one more trying ordeal awaited them, and many would not survive.

Alexander ordered a small fleet built and placed it under the command of one of his Companions, an officer named Nearchus. The ships were to sail west on the Arabian Sea so that Nearchus could see if the coastline extended up into the Persian Gulf or directly into Arabia and Africa. Nearchus was also expected to learn what harbors, gulfs, islands, and settlements existed along the coast—and to find out if the land nearby was fertile or barren.

The voyage would be a long one, and since the ships could carry only ten days' rations and a five-day store of water, Nearchus' supplies would have to be replenished frequently. To accomplish this, Alexander proposed to lead a body of troops along an inland route that was roughly parallel to the one taken by Nearchus. Then periodically he would have his men dig wells and establish food depots to resupply the fleet.

After sending the bulk of his army back to Persia by a northern route that skirted the desert in southern Pakistan, Alexander set out on what was to be his last great march. Of the force of twenty thousand that accompanied him, a large portion were women and children and other civilian camp followers whom he probably should have sent by way of the safer northern route. It was September, 325, and almost from the

first day of the march Alexander's men and their followers suffered from the extreme heat and felt the
short supply of food and water. After they had traveled
along the coast for about a hundred miles, the rugged-
ness of the terrain forced them to turn inland.

Now in the trackless desert their sufferings became
acute. There were long periods in which they traveled
without water. And when water was found, there was
only enough to supply a small caravan. The horses
and other beasts of burden were the first to drop.
Thirsty soldiers butchered them and drank their
blood—and then, ravenously hungry, began killing
the animals that still survived. Soon children were
falling behind, and women too. And many of the men
who fell out of line were lost forever. Alexander's
once disciplined army was now a half-crazed rabble,
frightened and fatigued. And Alexander, doubtless
suffering as much as they, must have been in despair.
But he kept on marching, and he continued sending
supply parties to the coast with a measure of what
remained of his dried meat and grain.

Somehow, after sixty days of wandering, the remnants of the host that had set out across the desert
staggered into the Persian royal residence at Pura.
Plutarch says that only a fourth of those who under-
took the trek survived it, but later historians generally
agree that the casualty ratio was considerably lower.

After recuperating in Pura, the survivors moved
two hundred miles farther west to the vicinity of
present-day Bandar Abbas on the Iranian south shore.
Here they were joined by the troops that had traveled

in relative comfort along the northern route. And soon, to Alexander's relief, Nearchus and his ships arrived. All but four were intact, and most of his men had survived—no doubt because during the frequent landings they had augmented what supplies they had found with fresh dates and the nutritious hearts of date palm leaves. And sometimes they had killed and eaten camels.

Now Alexander moved on toward Susa. He arrived there in the spring of 324—and in good time too, for his empire had not been functioning well in his absence. Corruption was in evidence and disorder reigned. His longtime friend Harpalus, who was the royal treasurer, had spent a fortune on riotous living and then had fled westward with as much of the treasury as he could carry. Now he was bribing Demosthenes and other Athenians to revolt. In Macedon, Olympias had been using her power to raise a faction against Antipater, making a stable government there impossible. Throughout the empire, military commanders had been robbing public buildings like buccaneers, and provincial satraps had been raising their own armies and muttering earnestly about revolt. Worst of all, the Macedonians in Persia were close to mutiny.

Alexander replaced many of the Persian satraps with Macedonians and dealt with dissidents in his usual way: a show of force, numerous threats, many killings. Despite the confusion felt throughout the empire, he continued to act as its all-powerful, dictatorial Great King.

In the spring of 324 he strengthened this position by marrying two women at the same time. One was Darius' daughter Statira, who had been captured with her mother and grandmother after the battle of Issus. The second wife he took in the same ceremony was Parysatis, daughter of Artaxerxes III, who had occupied the Persian throne before it was usurped by Darius III. Parysatis may have been in her early teens, Statira in her early twenties. Alexander chose Statira as his reigning queen, but by also marrying Parysatis he was able to unite the rival branches of the old Persian royal family. He was still married to Roxana, incidentally, although the ancient authorities do not mention her again until after Alexander's death.

In Alexander's great marriage ceremony at Susa, eighty of his chief officers took brides from among the daughters of Persian noblemen—including Hephaestion, who married Statira's younger sister Drypetis. Writes Arrian, "These weddings were solemnized in the Persian fashion: chairs were placed for the bridegrooms in order; then after the health drinkings the brides came in, and each sat down by the side of her bridegroom; they took them by the hand and kissed them, the King setting the example, for all the weddings took place together." Arrian reports that more than ten thousand Macedonian soldiers took Asian wives at this time, "and to all Alexander gave wedding gifts."

Despite the many marriages, the Macedonians were determined not to be absorbed into the culture of Persia. They consistently refused to emulate Alexander in adopting Persian dress and manners. And more and more they came to resent his apparent preference for Persian customs and his dependence on Persian troops.

This resentment turned into cold hostility when Alexander sent word to every Greek state except Macedon—where people would have been shocked by the insult to Philip's memory—that henceforth he must be recognized as the son of Zeus-Ammon. It is logical to assume that Alexander's proclamation of his divine status to the Greeks was, just as it had been to the Egyptians, a political measure taken to achieve a political purpose. As king of Macedon and captain-general of Greece, Alexander could not rightly intervene in the politics of the autonomous Greek states. But as the son of a god he could justifiably wield his absolute power over all the states and satrapies of his empire.

To his Macedonian soldiers, Alexander's actions at this time were the cause of suspicion and mounting discontent. "Alexander was not trying to oust the Macedonians from their ancestral partnership with him," explains Tarn, "but they thought he was." Their discontent flared openly when Alexander announced that ten thousand veterans could go home to Macedon. This announcement, combined with Alexander's obvious desire to unify the races of his empire, indicated to his troops that he might be planning to transfer the seat of power from Macedon to Asia—and they became angry.

At first they listened to him in silence, looking sullenly at one another. Then when he had finished, they burst into an uproar, mocking him and jeering and insisting that if any of them went home they would all go together.

Furious, Alexander leaped among them and ordered his guardsmen to seize and execute the men he singled out as ringleaders. Then he climbed back on the platform and in an impassioned speech reproached his men for their ungratefulness. According to Tarn's translation, Alexander concluded by shouting: "And now, as you all want to go, go, every one of you, and tell them at home that you deserted your king who had led you from victory to victory across the world, and left him to the care of the strangers he had conquered; and no doubt your words will win you the praises of men and the blessing of heaven. Go!"

Now his men stood in humble awe of their leader as he sprang down once again and strode to his quarters. There he remained for two days, sulking, refusing to see anyone. On the third day, when his officers and soldiers heard that he was replacing Macedonian commanders with Persians, they became panic-stricken. They knew they had offended him. Now, fearing the effect of his wrath, they came to his quarters and in tears begged to be forgiven. According to Tarn, one man cried out, "You have made Persians your kinsmen." And Alexander replied, "But I make you all my kinsmen." At this the soldiers cheered, and Alexander wept and forgave them. Then he held a great fraternization banquet for everyone—Macedonians and Persians, and representatives of all the races in his vast empire.

Another mutiny had been quelled. But this time it was Alexander who triumphed. He had stubbornly imposed his will on the men and had made concessions to none.

In late summer of 324 personal tragedy struck Alexander: Hephaestion fell ill and died at Ecbatana. Alexander was frantic in his grief over the loss of the friend he had come to consider his "twin." His mourning lasted for months. As one expression of his bereavement, he ordered the building of a huge sepulcher to Hephaestion in Babylon.

There are many indications that Alexander may have lost the will to live after Hephaestion's death. Although he proposed to conquer Arabia and lead an expedition around Africa, his plans seem to have been halfhearted. He had been weakened by battle wounds and worn out by constant marching, and now he seems to have become vigorously intent on self-destruction. More and more his drinking bouts and carousings were becoming prolonged, notorious affairs. Plutarch says that in the spring of 323 when Alexander arrived in Babylon to worship at Hephaestion's unfinished sepulcher, he "gave himself up to sacrificing and drinking." One night he drained a huge goblet containing six quarts of wine, and the next night he became drunk again, and the next night too.

Early in June, shortly before he planned to begin his Arabian expedition, he caught a cold, and soon a fever set in. At first there was no fear for his life, but in the stifling heat of the Babylonian summer his fever increased relentlessly, and he grew weaker and weaker.

Although the nature of his illness is unknown, it is likely that the cold and fever presaged the onset of malaria and a liver infection. On the sixth day of his affliction he was no longer coherent enough to give orders to his generals; on the ninth day he was speechless. Then word spread that his death was near.

Foremost in everyone's mind must have been the question of what would become of the empire when and if he finally died. Not even his wisest astrologers could have foreseen the widespread chaos that would ensue.

Contenders for the crown, writing a new chronicle in blood, would dispose of one another until the empire collapsed, splitting into five parts—each one under the administration of one of Alexander's generals. Lysimachus would seize Thrace, Antipater would take Greece and Macedon; Antigonus, Asia Minor; Seleucus, Babylonia; and Ptolemy, Egypt and Libya. It was Ptolemy who had Alexander's body transported to Egypt and placed in a mausoleum in Alexandria.

When the Greeks revolted against the Macedonians, Demosthenes would have a last moment of glory before Antipater struck at Athens and caused him to take poison. Aristotle was to die soon after Alexander—either from poisoning himself or from the exertions of his flight from Athens.

In Asia, Roxana, ever jealous of Alexander's queen, Statira, would arrange to have her murdered. And Roxana and a son born after Alexander's death would come under the care of Olympias. Fighting bitterly against the Macedonian faction led by Antipater,

Olympias and Alexander's sister eventually would be defeated and murdered. Then Roxana and her child would be put to death.

But no one could have foretold these tumultuous events as Alexander lay gravely ill in Babylon.

On the tenth day of his illness a rumor spread that he was already dead and that his death was being kept secret. Arrian reports that many of his men gathered at the palace, wanting to see their leader. They were allowed in finally, and passed through the pavilion where Alexander lay. "They say he was speechless as the army filed past," Arrian writes. "Yet he greeted one and all, raising his head, though with difficulty, and signing to them with his eyes."

The next day, when he was barely conscious, an officer leaned over him and asked to whom he would leave his empire. "To the best," Alexander reportedly whispered. And that evening he died, ending a reign of twelve years and eight months.

In his brief lifetime of less than thirty-three years, Alexander the conqueror had accomplished more than any man in history—and he had opened up a new world to Western culture. But Tarn points out that "he died with the real task yet before him; it remained to be seen if he could make peace. He had. . .opened up a new world; it remained to be seen what he could do with it."

He was, after all, only a man. To have accomplished everything he had set out to do, he probably would have had to be what he pretended—a god. His failings were real enough, and certainly Alexander himself was aware of them. But the key to his greatness can be seen clearly in what he tried and failed to do as well as in what he was able to achieve.

"For whatever else he was," says Tarn, "he was one of the supreme fertilizing forces of history. He lifted the civilized world out of one groove and set it in another; he started a new epoch; nothing could again be as it had been."

Did Alexander have a successor in mind when on his deathbed he mumbled, "To the best"? Probably not. But he obviously knew that if any one man could wrest the throne from the other would-be successors, that man would have to be "the best"—the strongest or the smartest of them. But no man was quite good enough.

Alexander had surrounded himself with many bright men, and strong men too; however, not for many generations would the world know one as strong, as brave, or as brilliant as Alexander the Great.

ACKNOWLEDGMENTS

"Alexander the Great Cutting the Gordian Knot" by Perino del Vaga courtesy Scala/Art Resource, New York.

Detail of mosaic of Alexander the Great on horseback courtesy Erich Lessing/Art Resource, New York.

Photo of Bouleuterion in Priene, Turkey, courtesy Vanni/Art Resource, New York.

Alexander the Great taming Bucephalus statuette courtesy Scala/Art Resource, New York.

"The Victory of Alexander the Great and the Construction of Alexandria" courtesy Cameraphoto Arte, Venice/Art Resource, New York.

Photo of coin depicting Alexander the Great as Heracles courtesy Erich Lessing/Art Resource, New York.

Photo of Lykian tombs in Xanthos courtesy Vanni/Art Resource, New York.

"The Entrance of Alexander the Great into Babylon" courtesy Giraudon/Art Resource, New York.

Mosaic of the battle between Alexander the Great and

King Darius courtesy Erich Lessing/Art Resource, New York.

"The Funeral Procession of Alexander the Great" courtesy Tate Gallery, London/Art Resource, New York.

"The Tent of Darius" courtesy Réunion des Musées Nationaux/Art Resource, New York.